JOINED

A Bench Guide to Furniture Joinery

Joshua A. Klein

Mortise & Tenon Inc.

SEDGWICK

Author
Joshua A. Klein

Editor
Michael Updegraff

Copy Editor
Megan Fitzpatrick

Photographer and Designer
Joshua A. Klein

Publisher
Mortise & Tenon

ISBN: 978-0-9983667-9-1

© 2020 Joshua A. Klein

All rights reserved. No part of this publication may be reproduced in any form or by any means including electronic and mechanical methods, without prior written permission from the publisher, except in the case of brief quotations in critical reviews and certain noncommercial uses permitted by copyright law.

Mortise & Tenon Inc.
14 Porcupine Ln
Sedgwick, ME 04676

www.mortiseandtenonmag.com

Printed and bound in the United States of America

Signature Book Printing
8041 Cessna Ave
Gaithersburg, MD 20879

www.sbpbooks.com

CONTENTS

Foreword 10

Introduction 12

The Square Mortise and Tenon 22

The Round Mortise and Tenon 70

The Through Dovetail 84

The Half-blind Dovetail 120

The Nailed Rabbet 132

The Dado 152

Afterword 170

Glossary 172

To Mitch Kohanek,
for teaching me to keep my goals always out of reach.

foreword

This is not a book for armchair woodworking.

Granted, there's nothing to stop you from thumbing through the pages while relaxing in a well-worn recliner, feet propped up after a long day. You can even read it in a swaying hammock on a warm tropical isle, or (less idyllically) from an uncomfortable perch in the back of the commuter bus. But *Joined* isn't at home there. This is a book meant for the workbench.

If you're anything like me, you get frustrated with the way most step projects are presented. Just do this, then do that, cut at this measurement, glue and clamp, and then boom! Your side table is done, and in only 32 easy steps! These are directions written for a machine to follow. Machinery only needs explicit commands, detailed measurements, and (quite importantly) featureless, uniform raw materials to work with. A machine can knock out 1,000 identical side tables, all perfect in their laser precision, no questions asked. But therein lies the big difference between us and machines. We want to ask questions. To learn.

See, machines don't grow in skill. They don't get better at the actions they practice, don't move from shaky beginner to confident master. They simply do as they are told, no more, no less. If they are programmed to bore a mortise in a specific location, they will do it all day (and all night, too). As long as the material is perfectly predictable, no jig slides out of adjustment, and no freak windstorm knocks out the power, the clone army of side tables will pour out the door and take over the neighborhood.

But introduce a variable – let's say, our maple tree had a branch on one side, once the home of a bird's nest. Imagine the tree was felled for lumber, the branch sawn off, and now we have a knot – a big loose one, right where our mortise needs to be. The machine does not ask questions – it will destroy the workpiece (and dull the cutting edge) in order to do what it is programmed to do. It can't adapt or adjust as needed to work with the materials, can't modify the design halfway through on a whim or because a creative impulse suggested something new. But humans *can* do that – we do it all the time. We're meant to.

This is a book about freedom. It's not about the "right" way to cut joinery; you won't find any measured drawings or prescriptions for dovetail angles listed here. What you will find is guidance on the skills necessary to execute the most commonly used joinery found in furniture, as well as a wealth of information on *why* each step is important and proceeds as it does. Joshua Klein has assembled this book to demonstrate and explain the vital aspects of each joint to enable the reader to move forward with confidence, adapting this knowledge to any new furniture situation. You won't just learn how to make a specific mortise-and-tenon joint for a specific application – you'll be free to adjust your plans and joinery for any size stock or project.

There are many good woodworking videos out there that can be helpful for learning techniques, but truth be told, bringing a smartphone, tablet, or laptop to the bench is not exactly ideal. Besides the fact that we use hand tools as a way of unplugging from modern technological frivolities (not to invite them to the party), these devices aren't built with workshop-ruggedness in mind. Drop your tablet on the floor, spill coffee on it, or throw it across the room in frustration at yet another life insurance ad, and you're out of luck. But the book you're holding is intended to find a home at the bench. Spilling coffee on it is no big deal – coffee stains make for nice patina. There's plenty of room in the margins for notes. You can even use it to swat at an annoying fly – try doing that with your iPad. In short, this may turn out to be one of the most practical books you own.

Working with hand tools isn't a practice focused solely on the end product. We take pleasure in the journey – admiring the beauty of freshly planed wood, feeling the satisfying bite of a sharp backsaw, driving a tenon home with one final acoustic tap. The delight we experience in these moments has nothing to do with ingenious programming, or a project's computer-generated flowchart. Instead, we appreciate the joy of working in concert with natural materials and simple tools to make something beautiful. Author Pearl S. Buck wrote, "To know how to do something well is to enjoy it." This book will be a valuable guide for you on that journey.

– Michael Updegraff
October 8, 2020

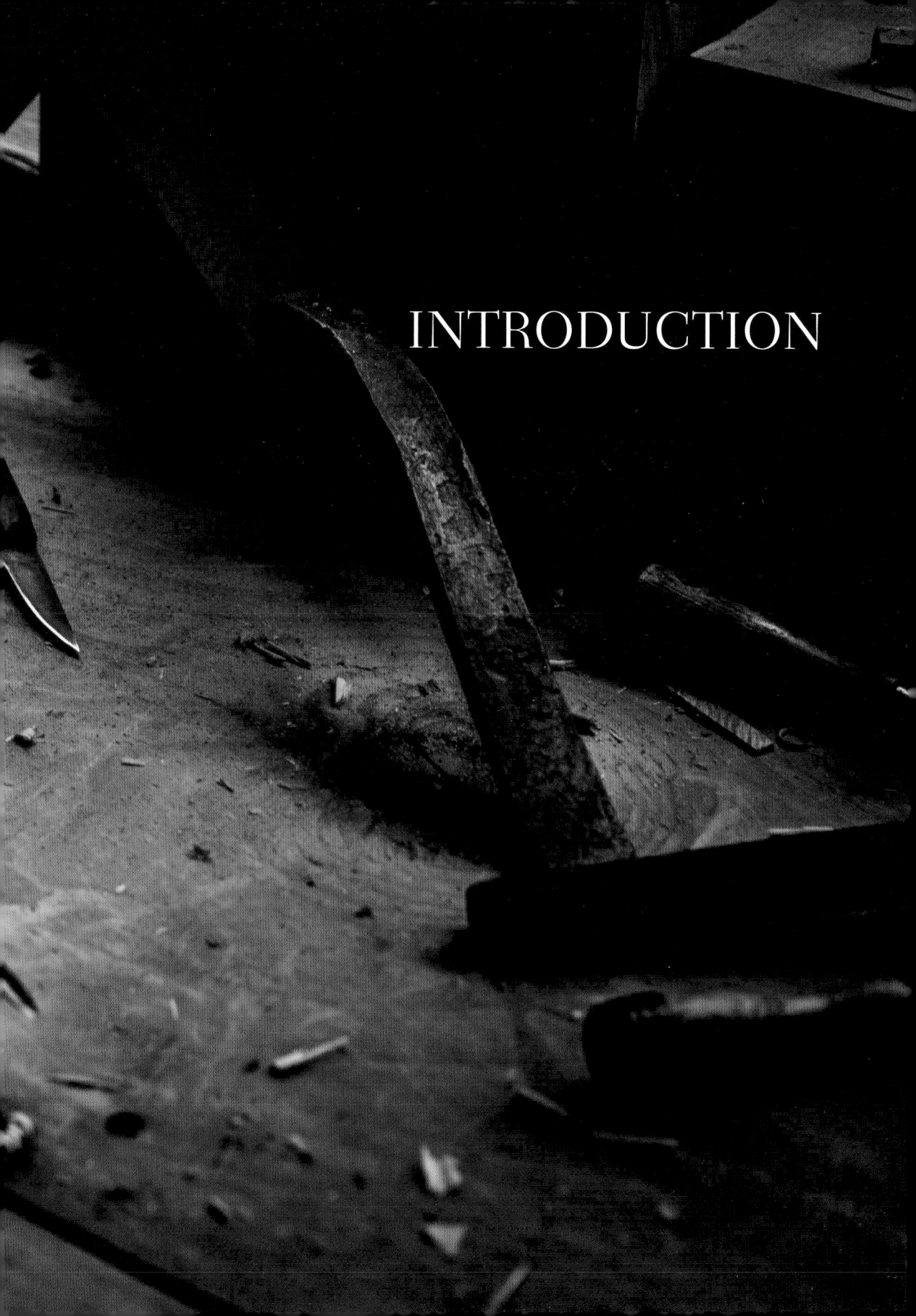

INTRODUCTION

"It's magic," they say.

Mitch Kohanek labored for nearly 40 years at the National Institute of Wood Finishing to teach his students the disciplines of furniture finishing and repair. He always set the bar out of reach, and nudged each of his pupils along to success. His belief in the value of diligent practice transpired in every lesson he taught, whether it was splicing new wood onto damaged chair parts or carefully blending dyes and pigments to make a wood fill seamlessly disappear. Year after year, Kohanek taught his students how to repair furniture in a way that inspired awe from onlookers – they always called it "magic." But his constant rejoinder came to be that in his school, "There are no tricks; there are only techniques." Kohanek's distinction between "tricks" and "techniques" became a hallmark of his teaching.

Most folks look for "tricks" when they don't want to learn any more information than is required to meet the immediate need. Tricks appeal to us because they do not entail discipline, diligence, or patience.

But craftspeople are never satisfied with this. They are the ones who acquire and develop "techniques" – methods based on observation and refined application. Their success relies on a holistic understanding of how each little step relates to the final result.

Kohanek emphasized that the skilled application of proven and appropriate methods is the mark of a skilled craftsperson, but he also taught that it's better to learn *why* each step is done, rather than to naïvely trust or disregard the instruction. It is when this depth of knowledge is acquired that we are empowered to successfully deviate from convention.

This is a book of techniques, not tricks. My primary goal here is to show you all the details in a way that helps you to develop a holistic understanding of fundamental furniture joinery.

Historic joinery is a fascinating subject because precision in some areas is absolutely essential (such as tight shoulders), while others areas are completely inconsequential (such as the insides of rails).

Pre-industrial joinery is puzzling to modern woodworkers. They see every shoulder tight and every surface polished on the outside, but can't understand how the underside can look so coarse. This workmanlike approach is particularly manifest in *Mortise & Tenon Magazine*'s photo examinations, which demonstrate time and again that pre-industrial craftsmen knew what mattered and strove for perfection in those details, but everything less vital was done as swiftly as possible. I will be approaching the joinery in this book in the same spirit. So pay close attention to what matters and what doesn't. If a step doesn't make sense, hang in there and keep going. Through practice, you'll begin to see the bigger picture.

Practicing these skills is essential, but don't waste time on practice for practice's sake. There are emerging woodworkers out there who spend precious shop hours rehearsing joinery on small mock-up joints, but I've never been a big fan of this approach. To my mind, if you're going to cut four dovetail joints, you might as well make a simple box. Not only will you end up with a finished product, but all of your practice will be contextualized. It is precisely this big-picture vantage point that will show how these joints work together and why they work the way they do.

The success of your woodworking effort is directly proportional to your ability to create a fine cutting edge. So don't underestimate the value of sharpening. Before you begin your project, take a bit of time to touch-up the edges of your tools.

Lastly, a word of warning, reader: Because you are human, you *will* make mistakes. It's life. But don't let failure discourage you – we can't leave *everything* to the experts. To paraphrase Gilbert Keith Chesterton, if a thing is worth doing, it's worth doing poorly first. You cannot expect that your first dovetails will be gap-free.

But your next box will be better.

Animal Hide Glue

In my mind, there is only one adhesive suitable for furniture joinery: animal hide glue. Hide glue granules can be purchased in a variety of "gram weight strengths," the most common being 192, 251, and 315. The ideal strength for joinery is 192 gram strength. Why wouldn't we want to use a higher gram strength version? The primary reason is that the higher the gram strength, the more water must be absorbed to achieve full hydration. All that extra water means that there will be substantial shrinkage as the glue dries. As counterintuitive as it sounds, Donald Williams, Smithsonian Institute Senior Furniture Conservator, maintains that because of this extreme shrinkage "higher gram strength glue may not yield the strongest glue line." Williams believes that 192 gram strength is best-suited to furniture joinery. I recommend picking up the "high clarity" variety – it's light colored and doesn't smell like a wet dog.

The only equipment you'll need is a double-boiler glue pot. There are two viable options: a commercially available electric glue pot ($$$) and a Crock-Pot from the local thrift store. I've always used a Crock-Pot and cannot think of a reason to fork up the

extra cash for the real deal. The little black fondue pot pictured above at left cost me $3.00. The cast-iron pot pictured at center was designed to be heated over a fire. The big pot is filled with water and the inner pot holds the glue. This style was used for a long time in pre-industrial cabinetmakers' shops, but I've heard too many stories about those shops burning down to start lighting fires in my woodshop. I'm sticking with my Crock-Pot.

Why Use Hide Glue?

There are many good reasons to use hide glue. Here are a dozen:

1. It's reversible with warm water.

This is critical for safe repair in the future. Adhesives that cannot be dissolved after curing present great danger to joinery when it comes time to disassemble it for repair. All adhesives fail after a while. So when that chair gets wobbly and needs to be reglued, the whole thing has to come apart, which always involves disassembling joints in which the glue bond has not been compromised. But how do you gracefully "reverse" an epoxied joint? You see the problem. When "the glue is stronger than the wood," and the glue cannot be dissolved, things are liable to start breaking. Until the development of synthetics in the 20th century, all furniture was glued with hide glue. To disassemble these pieces, a simple injection of warm water into the joint softens the bond and allows the restorer to slide the joint apart.

If you want your furniture to last longer than 20 years, use hide glue.

2. It adheres to old hide glue.

Because hide glue softens when introduced to warm water, a fresh application will soften the old for proper adhesion. This is important when regluing a joint because glues need to penetrate the surface of the wood in order to make a proper bond, and if a synthetic has sealed the surface, you will have a hard time getting adequate adhesion. Fresh glue applied over old synthetic glue is a crapshoot.

3. It's easy to manipulate the working properties.

"Hot hide glue" (i.e. unmodified), when heated to 140°F, has a very short open time. Depending on ambient temperature and humidity levels, we're talking a minute or two. The glue gels before drying, so everything needs to be set in short order. There are so many factors that change hide glue's working properties. You can extend the open time by turning the heat up in the room or using a heat gun on the members of the joint – chilly substrates gel hide glue almost instantly. But if you need at least 30 minutes of open time, you make "liquid hide glue" by adding salt or urea prills to the mix. There are commercial versions available, such as Patrick Edwards' "Old Brown Glue" and Titebond's "Genuine Hide Glue." Patrick's a great guy and makes a great glue, but I prefer to make my own because it's dirt cheap and so stinking easy. I've included my recipe at the end of this section.

There are other useful additives such as glycerin, which reduces fracturability of the glue, and alum, which makes it waterproof. The list goes on. Hide glue is a delightful rabbit hole.

4. It's inexpensive.

Several years ago, I bought 50 lbs. of granules from Eugene Thordahl at Bjorn Industries (http://bjornhideglue.com) for $5.00 a pound. I am able to mix it fresh whenever I need it and this will last for at least 20 years of professional work. Thordahl also sells granules in 1-, 5-, and 10-lb. increments.

5. It lubricates the joint instead of seizing it at assembly.

Dry-fitting is one thing, but as soon as you apply glue, you've got a whole new scenario. When yellow glue is applied to the mating members of a joint, the wood swells and the joint no longer closes tight like it once did. Hide glue, however, makes a well-fitted joint slide right into place without much force. Things I say in the following chapters, such as "when in pine, leave the line," assume the use of hide glue. If you're using yellow glue, you'll need to make a looser fit or you'll run into trouble at assembly time.

6. It is self-clamping.

As hot hide glue dries, it gels, which actually makes clamping unnecessary in some cases. This is handy when small bits need to be repaired, such as veneer chips or carvings. This is also how boards have been edge glued throughout history. Craftsmen planed the edges straight and square, applied the hide glue to both sides and rubbed them together for a few moments until the gel action set in. Then the pieces were set aside to let it self-clamp. It's magic. No, wait... it's just a technique.

7. It is easy to clean up after it dries.

Glue-covered fingers, glue-splattered pants, and drops and drips on your shoes are easily taken care of even long after it has dried. How? You guessed it: warm water or saliva. (You think I'm kidding.) I think this point is vastly underestimated. I recently lost my good sense and decided to use yellow glue on something (don't worry – not joinery!) and not only did it swell the wood, making assembly a nightmare, but I had glue-covered fingers and nearly got glue on my clothes. I had forgotten how careful I have to be with that stuff, because there's no way it's coming out in the wash. I've gotten so laid back over all the years of using hide glue that I forgot how much I despise yellow glue. Lesson learned.

8. It's incredibly strong.

Depending on your mixture and gram strength, hide glue is one of the strongest adhesives, and has been used for thousands of years to assemble wooden objects seeing heavy use.

9. But it's not too strong.

This is the Goldilocks principle. Sure, you want strong glue, but you don't want it too strong. If your furniture ever crashes to the floor, you don't want your joinery to be the thing to break – you want it to be the glue line, don't you? This concept of the "sacrificial component" is used in all astute designs. You may recognize this component as a fuse in an electrical system or a shear pin in a machine. When excessive current or force is inflicted, the failure of this component prevents damage to the rest of the system. Why snap off a tenon when you can let the glue fail instead? Pass up any glue marketed to be "stronger than wood." That's not what you want in your joinery.

10. It's a renewable resource.

Cows always make more cows. That isn't changing anytime soon.

11. It's safe for your health.

Cow protein is safe for humans. I've tasted it. OK, that's weird – don't taste it. But the point is that you can and that you aren't breathing toxic epoxy fumes in your woodshop.

12. It's got historic precedent.

Hide glue has been found in the furniture of Egyptian tombs (built 30 centuries ago), and it was the standard adhesive until the advent of synthetics in the mid 20th century. When something has been used all over the world for most of recorded history, I'd say it's worth considering.

Mixing & Storing

When I am not using the glue, I store the jar in the refrigerator where the batch can last more than a month without developing mold on top. If it does, I just wipe the mold off the gelled glue with alcohol. A little mold will not harm the glue's integrity. Historically, the glue pot sat out in the craftsman's workshop for months on end. It must have been quite stinky and probably began to lose its integrity at some point. Keep it in the fridge and you'll be fine. I usually start the glue warming in the Crock-Pot a couple hours before big glue-ups, or if I'm short on time, I will heat the jar in the microwave in 10-second increments. I never nuke it longer and walk away because the goal isn't to cook the glue, it's merely to warm it. If it bubbles, you're cooking it.

My Liquid Hide Glue Recipe

1. Mix in a small jar:
   1/2 cup hide glue granules
   2 tsp salt
2. Add 1/2 cup water.
3. Stir and let it soak overnight.
4. Heat in a double boiler at 140°F for at least 2 hours.

Making your own liquid hide glue is as easy (and quick) as making a bowl of oatmeal. It does not require a huge list of exotic ingredients, a digital scale, or an expensive double-boiler system. You need a clean jelly jar, a set of kitchen measuring cups and spoons, and a Crock-Pot. Oh, and a funnel makes pouring easier. Grab your granules and your salt and you're ready to get mixing.

Pour 1/2 cup of 192 gram strength hide glue into the jar.

INTRODUCTION 19

Add 2 teaspoons of salt. Don Williams has advised the use of non-iodized salt, which is marketed as "canning" salt. Stir the salt into the granules.

Pour 1/2 cup of water over the glue mix. If you are picky, avoid using city water with all its chemicals. There is no evidence I'm aware of that chlorine in these levels has ever caused adhesion problems, but who knows when the chemical cocktail will change? I wouldn't trust it. My well water at home is super clean stuff, so I don't bother tracking down purified water for my glue.

Stir the mixture so that all of the granules have access to the water. Leave it to sit with the lid on to let the granules fully absorb the water. Ideally, you'd leave it overnight.

The next morning, the granules will have absorbed the water and the whole thing will be a gelatinous blob.

Place the jar (with the lid on) into your glue pot. Add water in the glue pot to just below the level of the glue in the jar. Turn the pot on for at least 2 hours. The pot should be heating at 140°F. If your Crock-Pot has multiple heat settings, you will have to do a trial run with a thermometer to see which setting is closest to 140°F. The most important thing is that you don't cook your glue. Bubbling glue is a bad sign – that is too hot.

Stir the glue at regular intervals during the heating process to make sure everything is evenly heated.

The second time you heat this glue, it will be even more coalesced.

THE SQUARE
MORTISE AND TENON

The mortise-and-tenon joint has been around for thousands of years. The earliest example I'm aware of is from a wooden well in Germany that is more than 7,000 years old. It is the joint that ties together Europe's cathedrals and the one that every antique table is designed around. Although the mortise-and-tenons in timber frames are almost identical to the joint I teach you here, the difference in scale makes the construction process quite different. For now, we're focusing on furniture-scale joinery.

The joint we will be making in this chapter is for a table, but cabinetmakers' chairs, bed frames, and some styles of chests typically incorporate mortise-and-tenon work. The knowledge required to cut the joinery for those forms is all contained within this lesson.

We're starting here because this joint offers the opportunity to exercise just about every different skill you'll need to develop to cut joinery of *any* type: careful layout using reference faces, sawing to a line, precision paring, direct transferring of dimensions onto the mating member, eyeballing short distances, etc. The bulk of the skills you'll learn in this chapter will serve as the foundation for the rest of the chapters. Once you've grasped the joints here, you'll find all of the infinite variations in the big, wide world to be a breeze. You'll look at a joint or a drawing of it, and instantly see what's different and what you have to do to make it.

Lay this book on your bench and open your tool chest – it's time to get to work.

The mortise-and-tenon joint is completely designed around one particular tool: the mortise chisel. This "pigsticker," as some like to call it, has a long track record in the woodworking trades. The chisel pictured here is a modern, precisely manufactured recreation of a traditional English design. It is a stout tool designed just as much for prying as it is chopping.

The mortise chisel width determines the width of the mortise and its corresponding tenon. For general furniture work, I use 3/8". I also own a 1/4" mortise chisel, but don't recall ever having used it on a project. Antique examples of this tool are rarely exact in width, but it doesn't make any difference because the double-pinned mortise gauge is set to match the chisel, whatever its measurement. I modified a retired antique gauge by installing and filing two small brad nails. I sharpened them to cut at the exact width of the chisel, but these nails are easy to bend with pliers for micro adjustments. Once the pins are set, that gauge and that chisel are life-long partners.

We'll be cutting the tenon first, but it doesn't really matter which goes first because both mortise and tenon are cut to match the mortise chisel width. I'll be demonstrating how to join a table rail to a leg, but all mortise-and-tenon joints share the same steps. Determine the exterior face of your rail stock – this is the surface that you will always reference your gauge off of. *At no point* in this process should you be gauging off the inside face. In hand work, the coarse tool marks left inside make precision impossible from that face. Set the gauge pins to be centered on the rail stock. Lock the fence and scribe the double lines a couple inches down the edge, across the end grain, and a couple inches on the bottom edge.

Notice the gauge lines are parallel to the exterior face on the left. The inside face on the right is not a perfectly consistent thickness, especially at the top. This doesn't affect anything because nothing is ever referenced off that face.

Now, lay the rail on the leg stock to determine the length of the tenon. A table really shouldn't have tenons shorter than 1-1/4", but the other factor to consider is the thickness of the material between the bottom of the mortise and the outside of the leg. I like at least 3/8" of buffer. Use your knife to stab a mark for the outside shoulder.

Lay the rail on a side rest (modern woodworking literature tends to call this a "bench hook") and carry that point square across the grain, denoting your exterior tenon shoulder. That line is what I call "sacred." Once established, you leave it pristine. It's the only place in the entire joint that will be seen after assembly. If it's marred or bungled, the joint will always look bad, no matter how precise the rest is. On the other hand, if this looks good, there's a mountain of grace for the other details. So scribe carefully with a sharp knife. Go slow and steady. I like to scribe three times, progressively deeper each time.

Turn the rail on edge and place your knife's edge into the scribed shoulder at the arris (corner). With your square referencing off the exterior face, slide the square against the knife blade. The physical registration of this method ensures a confident accuracy far better than squinting at a pencil line. Scribe square shoulders on the top and bottom edges from the front to the back. At this point, you can scribe the interior shoulder in the same manner. Don't bother with the careful deepening of the shoulder on the inside – it's not a show surface.

The shoulder now needs a V-groove for the saw to rest in. Using the corner of a chisel on the waste side of the line, gently remove the wood to the depth of your shoulder knife line.

I often skew the chisel to make sure I stay well clear of that sacred shoulder line. Don't push hard or into the shoulder, because if you slip, the sacred will become profaned.

If your knife line isn't quite deep enough for saw teeth to sit in, carefully scribe the shoulder deeper against the square's blade.

Using a finely toothed crosscut backsaw, place the teeth into the V at the far side of the tenon shoulder. Use your left thumb as a guide to prevent the teeth from jumping out onto the show surface. Because Western saws cut with full force on the push, begin by gently pulling the saw back toward you for a few teeth. This eases the start of the cut. If you don't have a solid kerf after one pull, repeat the backward stroke a few more times until you do.

Do the same on the near side.

LEFT, TOP: Slowly lengthen the kerfs by alternating between them until they meet in the middle. Once you have one continuous kerf, begin sawing down to the tenon's uppermost gauge line, but do so at a slight angle, tilting the teeth into the shoulder in order to give it a slight undercut. You'll see why this is significant as the joint develops.

RIGHT, TOP: Once the kerf is deepened to the tenon, you'll see the knife-crisp shoulder line on the left side and the coarseness of the saw cut on the right.

LEFT, BOTTOM: Flip the rail over with the interior face up, and this time place the saw teeth directly on the shoulder line. Saw straight down to the tenon line without tilting the saw as you did on the show shoulder. This will result in the interior shoulder being half-of-a-saw-kerf shy of the layout line. This is ideal because it intentionally relieves this inside shoulder from the test-fitting scenario at the end.

RIGHT, BOTTOM: Notice how the exterior face (top edge as shown) is slightly undercut and the interior face was sawn straight down on the scribed line. Jump ahead to page 55 to see how this looks once assembled.

Before sawing the tenon free, place the rail on the leg to determine how much reveal you'd like to have. You can have the rail flush to the outside of the leg, but it is common to have it set in a bit. It looks nice, but it also has a practical side – you don't have to plane any high spots flush. Stab a mark at the tenon's outer gauge line.

Drop the outer gauge pin into the knife mark and lock the fence.

Scribe the mortise lines a little longer than the rail is wide. On antique furniture, it's expected to see these gauge lines continue on the leg a bit below the rail. They attest to the piece's handmade origin – don't try to stop the lines exactly at the bottom of the rail.

With the mortise scribed onto the leg, you can saw the tenon free. Place the rail in a front vise, turned 45° away from you. To begin sawing the cheeks with your tenon saw, it is handy to have a kerf to set the saw teeth in. Some folks carve a little V-notch on the edge next to the line, but I prefer to use a backward stroke of my saw. I place the teeth on the waste side of the line, tilt the teeth away from the line, and give a firm, short pull back. This leaves me with a good starting place to begin sawing.

The main benefit of tilting the rail 45° is comfort – your saw can remain parallel with the bench. But it also helps you keep an eye on both of the lines you're sawing to. The line on the edge and the line down the end grain are both important to keep an eye on. I have also sawn this in the other orientation (facing the bench with the rail held vertically), but I find planting my hip against the bench provides steadiness in the cut. It's akin to the way a tripod's three points of contact give more stability than two.

Looking down at the sawing progress – you are aiming to keep the kerf on the waste side of the line. Cut slowly and carefully so that you can watch both edge- and end-grain lines.

Once you're close to the far side, stop. Saw the second cheek in the same way.

Now flip the rail around and begin sawing from the other side to meet your kerf.

Turn the rail upright in the vise and carefully saw the V-shaped material that remains.

Once you've reached bottom, you'll meet the shoulder cut and the waste should fall free. If you didn't saw the shoulder quite deep enough, you might have to go back to deepen it. You should be able to notice the saw patterns on the first tenon cheek: There are two diagonal cuts that leave an upside-down V in the center. This gives a strong visual of the three stages of sawing it takes to rip the cheek.

Finish sawing the second cheek as you did the first.

As you approach the bottom of the rip, support the waste with your free hand so that the backsaw doesn't fall, marring the show face. Some folks prefer to rip the cheeks before crosscutting the shoulders, but I favor this way because I can see what's going on better. In reality, the order of these two cuts is immaterial.

If it looks like you've sawn all the way on both the rip and crosscuts but the waste has not fallen away, it means you have material hanging on in the middle. Use the front few teeth of your saw to focus attention on the middle of the cut.

Nine times out 10, the waste falls free in a few passes. Your tenon is now roughly formed.

We don't want the tenon to be the same height as the rail because its accompanying mortise would have to continue out the top of the leg, making a weaker joint. To prevent this, we have to trim the height of the tenon down a bit, a process 19th-century cabinetmaker and author Peter Nicholson called "haunching." I never measure the exact amount of haunching, but eyeball something like 3/8", sawing plumb without striking any lines. Even if it's not perfect, one pass with a paring chisel tidies it up. Always saw this line with the show face toward you so that you can see that sacred shoulder as you approach it with the saw. It would be disheartening to nick that crisp line you've sweat over.

Turn the rail horizontally in your vise, and use your crosscut backsaw to remove the little piece. Keep an eye out for your show shoulder.

JOINED: A BENCH GUIDE TO FURNITURE JOINERY

A 2"-wide chisel is the perfect tool to pare the high spots down to the tenon's gauge lines. Don't be tempted to put your non-dominant hand out in front of the chisel's edge. Keep it back as pictured here. Pay particular attention to the intersection of the shoulder and cheek saw cuts – it's not uncommon to find a bit of material to pare off.

The tenon doesn't have to look pretty; it just needs to fit the mortise.

Here is one reason I prefer to have my workbench against a wall: avoiding the use of clamps in paring operations. To pare chamfers onto the tenon for ease of assembly, I butt the rail against the wall. This is so much faster than messing with clamps or a vise and allows me to instantly adjust the workpiece.

A related technique is pinning the work with my hip into a fixed point on the bench. Depending on the stock's length, sometimes it's the metal-toothed bench hook (planing stop) or in this case the wooden side rest. I'm sure some would think this is silly and that I should really just put this thing in the vise, but each chamfer takes no more than 1 or 2 seconds and there's no way I'm going to adjust the stock in the vise between all of those cuts. My goal is swiftness.

The chamfers don't need to be huge – just enough to avoid getting hung up on errant junk in the mortise corners.

42   JOINED: A BENCH GUIDE TO FURNITURE JOINERY

Now that the tenon is trimmed to size, lay it on the leg to mark the top and bottom of the mortise. Stab these two marks with your knife. You will want at least an inch of material on the leg above the rail. This "horn" is extra material to provide strength during mortising.

Knife the top and bottom of the mortise square across the inside face. (If you have a reveal, you might want to avoid carrying the line all the way to the front, or it will be visible in the end.)

The finished layout of the mortise.

I encourage you to chop your mortises on a low bench or "mortising stool." Some folks like to do this up high at the regular bench, but the first time I tried this seated method I was blown away. To get up over your work makes a huge difference in speed and efficiency. Every time I've taught this method, no matter how much I've warned folks, someone inadvertently chops through the other side. If you have experience chopping mortises at the high bench, try this and you'll see what I mean.

I learned this method of mortising from a host of period documentation. I like to sit side-saddle on top of the work that is to be mortised. This enables me to stand up quickly and make adjustments. In the context of a whole build, I recommend laying all four legs together at the same time, because the extra width creates a much more comfortable seat. Being positioned over the work also enables me to sight down the chisel to make sure I'm chopping straight. Crooked mortises are a nuisance to deal with.

Begin chopping with the bevel toward you about 1/2" from the near side of the mortise. Rock the chisel side to side to align the edge within the gauge lines, then give it a confident rap with the mallet. This is your starting place.

Then back up somewhere between 1/8" and 3/16", depending on the hardness of the wood, and make another chop. This will likely pop the chip free.

Bring the chisel to the other side of the starting line with the bevel still facing you and chop down in a V.

Pry up with the tip of the chisel to remove the waste.

Return to the far side and continue chopping backward incrementally. Each step back should also deepen the V.

Pretty soon, every couple chops down will generate enough waste that you'll have to pry it out to watch your progress.

Alternate back and forth a few times, focusing on deepening the mortise. Just make sure that you leave at least 1/4" of material between the chisel and the lower edge of the mortise – we don't want to be prying there. Most woodworkers in the 18th and 19th centuries seemed to consider that spot sacred.

You can still pry safely as long as you have that 1/4" buffer.

As you get deeper, you can use two hands to pry, just don't be too aggressive or the upper edge of your mortise might chip. If it happens, it's not the end of the world, but it is an indicator that you're not working in a controlled way. Ease up on the prying. I aim to reach full depth once I'm two thirds of the way across the mortise.

To check for depth, I use my knife (always at the ready on my hip) to gauge the tenon. I lay the knife down to the shoulder and pinch with my fingers at the end of the tenon.

I then place it into the deepest part of the mortise to check depth. If you're shy of full depth, use this technique to measure your progress against the outside of the leg. That'll show how far you have to go.

Once you're in a groove, it's hard to change course – be watching to make sure your chisel stays straight in line with the leg. If the mortise is crooked, your chisel will show you.

Keep working backward all the way to the top of the mortise, not fearing to pry on that surface, because it will be hidden in the assembled joint. As you get to the top edge, chop a little bit of an undercut so that the top of the mortise is more than 90°. You don't need to go extreme here, but intentionally *exceeding* 90° ensures that you're not *shy* of 90°, which would definitely impede your tenon from fully seating.

Here's another benefit to the horn. I tap it on the bench to clear the chips out of the mortise. It doesn't matter if this gets beat up because it will be cut off eventually anyway.

When everything beyond your starting point is chopped to full depth, it's time to make your way to the bottom line. First, chop all the remaining sloped waste straight down to full depth before moving any closer to the line. Then begin to chop straight down in 1/8" increments until you are about 1/16" away from the line, but do not pry at all during this operation.

If there's too much material on the bevel side of the chisel, the bevel will drive the tool into your line as you chop. You can avoid this by doing two things: 1. Make sure that you have no more the 1/16" of material on the bevel side of the chisel. 2. Ever-so-gently cut a little shelf that your chisel can sit on. Then you can safely chop straight down to full depth.

The top mortise line (above, left) is pried upon, but will be hidden. The bottom mortise line (above, right) is sacred, so chop with the utmost care.

Below is what the bottom surface of the mortise looks like from the chisel. It is the absolute-least important area of an entire piece of furniture, and always looks like trash inside period mortises. The only consideration is that nothing gets in the way of the tenon.

If you've done accurate work to this point, final fitting is a quick task. The tenon should wiggle in with force, but you don't want it to drop in under its own weight. Don't forget to check the top and bottom of the tenon. To adjust the thickness, first make sure the exterior cheek is flat in plane with the gauge lines. Once it is, do not pare that cheek because that will change your reveal. Rather, all thicknessing must take place on the interior cheek. Work slowly and systematically, checking the fit every few passes.

Here's a close-up shot of a proper fit on the exterior shoulder – nice and crisp.

Here's the inside shoulder with its half-a-kerf gap.

This overhead view of the joint clearly illustrates the difference between the show surface fit (top) and the secondary surface fit (bottom).

THE SQUARE MORTISE AND TENON

Now that the tenon is fit, mark the top of the leg off the top of the rail. In the past, I've taught students to scribe this line early on when laying out the top and bottom mortise lines, but without fail, there's someone who starts daydreaming and chops all the way to the top of the leg. It's safer to mark this line once the joint is complete.

Now mark for the pins. Table tenons usually get two wooden pins. I never measure their top or bottom locations, but just eyeball at least 3/4" on either side, and about 3/8" from the shoulder. Mark and begin boring these holes with a square awl.

Put the leg in the vise and bore the 1/4" pin holes all the way through the leg.

Yes, the exit side will break out. No, it doesn't matter.

THE SQUARE MORTISE AND TENON

Snip off any fibers in the mortise with your knife and slide the tenon in to mark it with an awl. Make sure the shoulder is nice and tight and mark the tenon cheek. Ah, but wait! Don't mark it exactly in the center of the hole, instead, mark it in toward the shoulder a bit. That's right: *in toward the shoulder*. This subtle offset will force the shoulder tight when the pin is driven. This method is called "drawboring," and it frees you from having to use clamps for assembly. If you offset the holes the wrong way though, it will force your joint apart. Remember: *in toward the shoulder*.

How much offset should you use? It always depends on the scale of the joint and the wood species used, but in general I aim to put the point of the awl at about two thirds of the diameter of the hole (or a touch shy of that) as shown here. Do a few and you'll get the hang of it.

This back-and-forth test fitting and marking can get tedious, but it's important to never work blindly. It's always worth double checking and marking carefully so as not to spoil your hard work. To remove the tenon, press the leg firmly on the bench and wiggle the rail out without yanking. Also, keep your face away from the end of the rail when pulling it out. Don't ask how I know.

The tenon should show two clear points for boring.

Bore the tenon's pin holes, but be mindful to stay dead on target. Misalignment here makes a mess to fix later.

In hardwoods, a drawbore pin clears the way for the wooden pin.

Jam the pin into the holes to snug the shoulder tight. Check the alignment and fit before moving on. If you messed up your tenon holes, now's the time to fix them. Widen them or plug them and re-bore as needed. Don't fudge this alignment – if the shoulder isn't tight now, it won't be any tighter in 200 years when your great, great, great, etc. grandchildren inherit it. Make it right now.

I have a pile of bone-dry riven ash pin stock stashed under my workbench. Find some good, straight stuff like this. These blanks are about 4" long, dead straight, and split like a dream. Use a 2" chisel to split the stock in half and in half again until you have the size blanks you need.

Shoot for square-sectioned stock a little wider than 1/4".

I recommend you pare your pins at a little shop-made block like this. The shelf should be a little shorter than the pin length so that you can hold onto the end of the pin while paring – you don't want your fingers anywhere near the front of that chisel edge. First, clean the riven blank to an even square cross-section with a subtle taper in thickness. This will take a bit of unsure practice, but once you get used to it, you can do this in only a few passes. Don't worry about paring the end you're holding – it's just for grip now and hammering later. It will be cut off.

Make the tapered square a tapered octagon. It can be as perfect or haphazard as you like – there's historic precedent for either.

62 JOINED: A BENCH GUIDE TO FURNITURE JOINERY

Finally, point the tips so they slide in easily. Some woodworkers wonder why I don't use a dowel plate to make my pins. The first reason is that I'm not a big fan of the perfectly uniform look, but also in my experience it takes longer. In one class I taught, each of my 10 students needed 16 pins for their table. That's a lot of pins. The TA, Raphael Berrios, and I gave them a head start by making a bunch of them. After a while, Raphael wanted to see if the dowel plate was faster, but soon realized that it was slowing him down. Dowel plates still require a good amount of prep to get the blank small enough to drive into the plate. Basically, it just added one more step. Raphael ditched the plate after a few pins and went back to paring.

Here's how you want your pins to fit. You should be able to push them in by hand but not enough that they already come through the other side. It should take some hammering to get them to protrude.

THE SQUARE MORTISE AND TENON   63

It is worth taking a few minutes before an assembly to clean up tools and sweep the bench of chips and wood bits. It also pays to take the time to think through the whole process so that you're not missing anything. Successful assembly requires clear space and a clear head. Do a quick dry run to make sure you've got everything you need right at hand.

For every assembly, I recommend you lay out all your parts oriented in the way they will go together. You don't want to be fumbling or having to flip the pieces around while the glue is cooling. Panic and confusion makes most of us flustered enough to cause mistakes. Also, when I glue an assembly on my workbench, I lay a paper barrier down. As you can tell, I'm not concerned about the bench itself, but I am concerned about hard glue drops marring future projects. One time as I was working on a project, I kept finding the same dent-shape all over my work. I rubbed my hand all over the benchtop to find that hidden glue, but to no avail. And it kept appearing in new places. Just as I was fully agitated, I slipped my hand into my open vise, and wouldn't you know it, a big old glob of rock-hard glue – right in my vise chop. So, feel free to ignore my advice, but the first time to find a dent in your work from dried glue, don't say I didn't warn you.

JOINED: A BENCH GUIDE TO FURNITURE JOINERY

Take the jar of hide glue out of the pot and carefully apply the glue with a brush on both sides of the mortise.

Then, give both cheeks of the tenon an even coat of glue. Slide the tenon into the mortise, and rejoice that you're using hide glue and not PVA.

Grab your hammer and drive those pins. In hardwood, you don't need to be shy; just don't break the pin. If you're building with a softer wood, like pine, take it easy on the driving. If you go slow, you'll hear when you've hit too hard. In hardwood, you'll feel the pin just sort of stop as if it were continuous with the leg and rail. No need to go any further.

As you're driving, don't even look at how far the pin is protruding, because it doesn't matter. In my joint here they barely emerge, but sometimes they stick out more than an inch. I've seen the protruding pins of period tables dealt with in just about every conceivable way: from sawing them off willy-nilly, to paring them nice and flush, to breaking them off with a hammer, to leaving them alone to stick out in midair. The point is, it's all on the underside, so do whatever makes you happy. Depending on how the glue-up went, you might consider trying the hammer approach.

Saw the pins at the outside face of the leg as near to flush as you can manage with a fine saw, and pare them flush with a bevel-down chisel. Work your way around the circumference of the pin, paring in toward the center, otherwise you risk breaking grain off the back of the pin.

Finish the last paring cuts with the bevel up in a slicing motion to bring it in plane with the leg.

Once the hide glue squeeze-out has gelled, you can roll it off the surface. It can also be cleaned up with warm water, but why bother? Just wait a few minutes and it rolls right off.

The finished interior of a pre-industrial mortise-and-tenon joint.

The finished show face of the joint. After you cut the horn off all four legs, the tabletop has a place to sit.

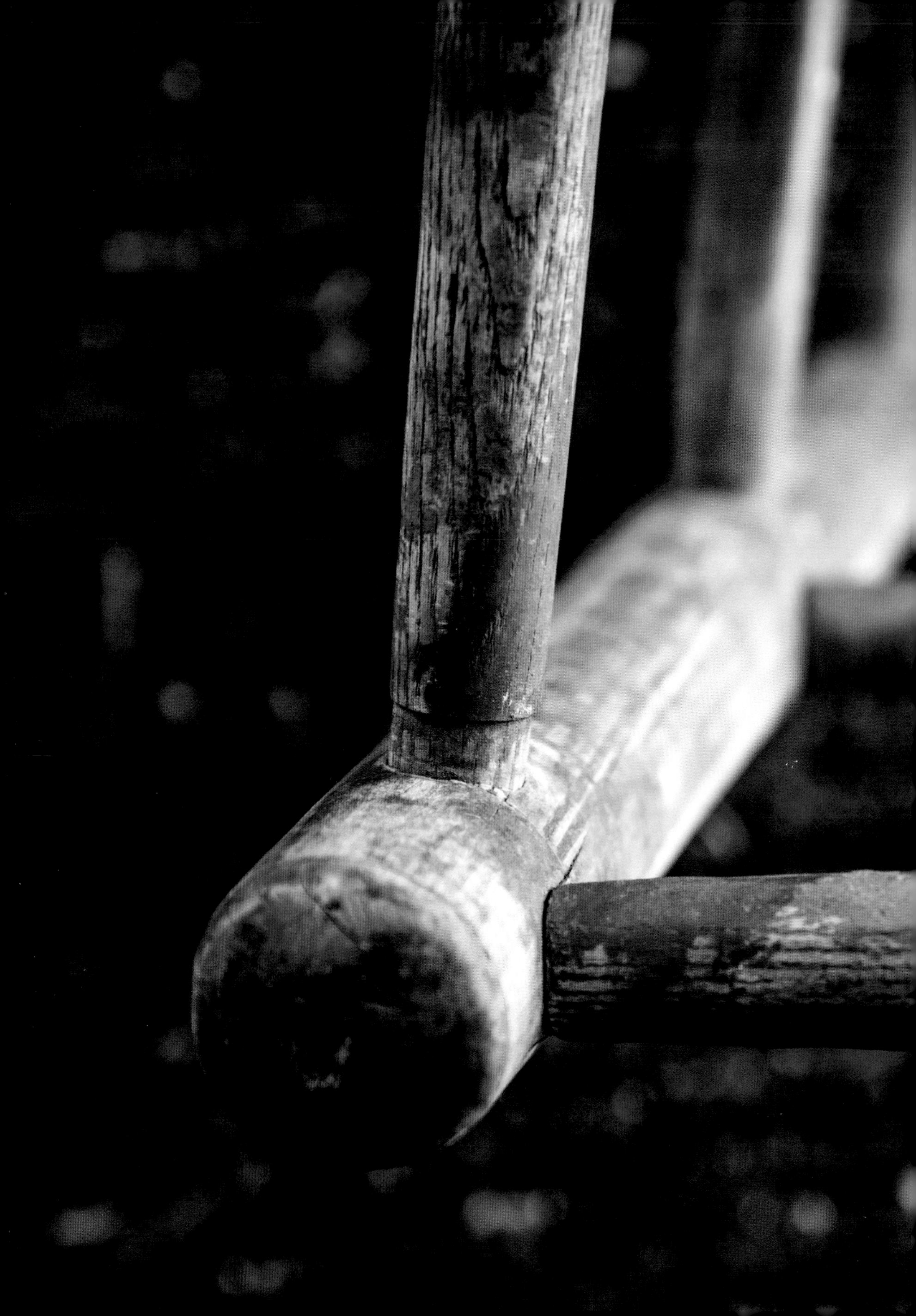

THE ROUND MORTISE AND TENON

Pre-industrial furniture makers' records show the chairs made by a turner were a fraction of the cost of the cabinetmakers'. This is a mystery to many when they first hear it. What accounts for the difference? Why are turned chairs so inexpensive relative to square-stock chairs? By the end of this chapter, you will know why. The 30 minutes you might have spent carefully chopping that square mortise will be replaced with 30 seconds of boring with a brace. All that careful layout of the tenon and the show face/inside face distinction will not be useful here, because the tenon will be formed in one fell swoop with another bit. You might just convert to chairmaking after this chapter.

The first step in making a round mortise-and-tenon joint is boring the mortise. We will be using an 11/16" auger bit which corresponds to the tenon-forming bit – I'll be introducing you to that tool below. Historic chair-rung tenons range in size, larger or smaller than ours here, but 11/16" is suitable for every round tenon you'd need for post-and-rung chairs. Only Windsors require additional gear.

These auger bits have small lead screws, which pull the bit deeper into the wood with each turn. Lead screws make it so you don't have to push hard to get the bit to bite. Put the leg to be mortised into your vise as perpendicular as possible to the benchtop. Begin by slowly turning the auger bit so that the cutters slice the round opening.

Once the mortise perimeter is cut, you can pick up the pace and bore to full depth. Count your turns – One handy feature of lead screws is that the depth relates more to the number of rotations, and less to the force applied. Once you've determined how many turns it takes to get to full depth for your project, simply repeat that number of rotations for each subsequent mortise. Once the perimeter was cut, it took me 20 rotations to get to my 1-1/16" mortise depth. Your mileage will vary.

As the boring proceeds, I recommend periodically checking your alignment with a square against the leg and by sighting from all directions. But I would encourage you to think of the square as training wheels, teaching your eye to see square and plumb in reference to your workbench top. Once you develop that skill, you won't need the square anymore. It's also valuable to know that, while we do want to do our best to keep dead-on, these mortises are not spoiled by basic human fallibility. If the mortise is a few degrees off, it will simply put the chair into a strengthening tension – not a bad thing. Many modern chairmakers use multiple machinist squares, angled mirrors, and lasers to achieve consistent angle perfection. At that point, it seems more logical to me to make a drill press jig.

I prefer to eyeball it.

THE ROUND MORTISE AND TENON

This is a 7/8" hole saw, which I use as a tenon-forming bit. This bit is used basically off-the-shelf with only slight modification: I remove some set from the inside of the bit by bending the teeth out with pliers. It took me 15 minutes of trial and error on scrap wood to dial it in to perfectly match my 11/16" bit. (Read on to learn of the "right" fit for this joint.)

To dispel the concerns of my naysayers, this is no modern cheater's "trick." The workshop of the Dominy craftsmen, now on display at the Winterthur Museum in Delaware, produced furniture on Long Island, N.Y. in the 18th century. They made the tenons of their chairs with a tool exactly like this. Their tenon-cutting bit looks like a piece of pipe fastened to a tapered wooden pad for a brace. The end of the pipe has saw teeth filed onto it in exactly the same way mine does. There is nothing new under the sun.

The stretcher stock should not be larger in diameter than the outside set of the hole saw's teeth, otherwise you won't see the shoulder while boring. In this case, I wanted a prominent stretcher shoulder, so I shaped the stretcher to be just the thickness of the bit. If you don't want such a hard, prominent shoulder, just shave it a little smaller.

To get the bit started on center, chamfer the end of the stretcher with your knife. Work systematically around the circumference, making an even chamfer. Keep your non-dominant hand out of the way of the edge, and use that thumb to push the back of the knife blade into the cut. The handle should largely stay put to function as a fulcrum point in this kind of slicing cut.

THE ROUND MORTISE AND TENON

The chamfer should be even enough to guide the bit, but doesn't have to look attractive.

Press the tenon bit onto the chamfer and rotate it to start a centered kerf.

Chuck the bit into your brace and begin cutting. Use the shoulder of the stretcher as your guide to keep things straight as you go.

I have a nick filed onto my bit to function as a depth gauge to determine the 1" length of the tenon. The little windows on this bit make seeing progress a snap.

If you're making a shouldered tenon, you'll have fuzz like this hanging out.

Slice the fuzz off the shoulder with your knife in this "can opener" grip. Roll the knife edge around the circumference in a slow, steady manner.

78   JOINED: A BENCH GUIDE TO FURNITURE JOINERY

Before driving the tenon, chamfer the end with a knife.

The tenon should fit crazy tight and only partway with hand pressure. If it can be forced in all the way by hand, it's too loose.

Now, your tenon is bigger than the mortise, and that's good – but you don't want to split the leg when you drive it. Carve shallow flats on the two sides perpendicular to the grain orientation of the leg (i.e. the "sides" of the tenon, not the "top" and "bottom"). This sideways relief ensures that your tenon doesn't act as a wedge, splitting the leg apart. This was a common historical practice.

Brush a little hide glue in the mortise then dip the end of the tenon in hide glue.

Drive it in. Hard. This joint is a serious mechanical lock so it ought to be a bear to assemble. If you're not scared the first few times doing this, it's not tight enough. One period chairmaker recorded a particular day's shop work with this intriguing note: "Worked upon a chair; broke it putting it together. Began another." Period chairmaking is not for the milquetoast.

It goes without saying: You'll want to make a handful of mock-ups before attempting this maneuver on an actual chair project.

The proper amount of glue will yield a small bead of squeeze-out. Let the squeeze-out gel and roll it off the surface without smearing it into the wood. If it accidentally smears, wipe it down with warm water.

THE ROUND MORTISE AND TENON

So, what if you don't want to use the tenon-cutting bit? Is there another way to form a round tenon without a specialized tool? Of course there is – you can simply carve it with your knife. It's just a bit more finicky.

Lay out the tenon diameter with the bit itself by placing the lead screw on the center of the tenon and gently boring until you scribe the circumference.

This is your guide line to carve to.

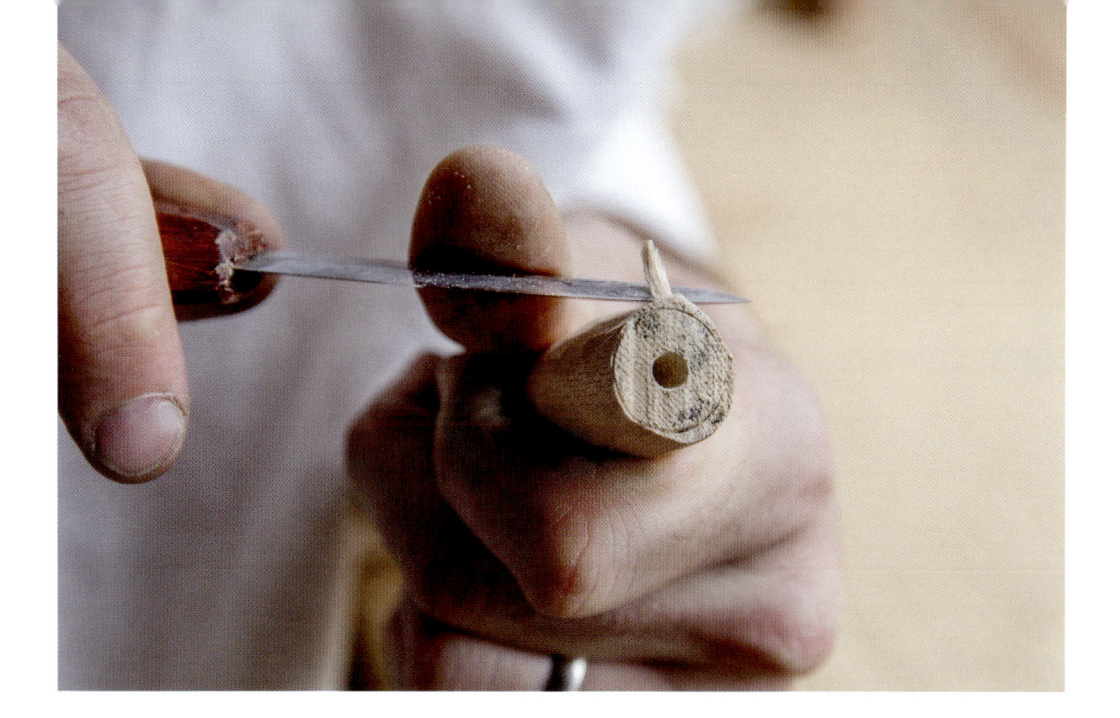

Take a slice with your knife, again pushing with your thumb, then rotate the stretcher for the next slice. Working systematically like this goes a long way in creating uniformity in the tenon. If you take off random chunks willy-nilly, you're going to have a hard time forming a tenon that fits tightly all around.

You can carve a shoulder if you want, but here's another option for a less-refined look. The facets on this tenon are suitable enough for a good glue joint, so don't try to make it perfectly smooth all around. The trick with this method is about making a regular cylinder of consistent thickness the whole way down. Each tenon needs to be carefully checked before final assembly. This method is picky and slow; that's why I prefer the tenon bit.

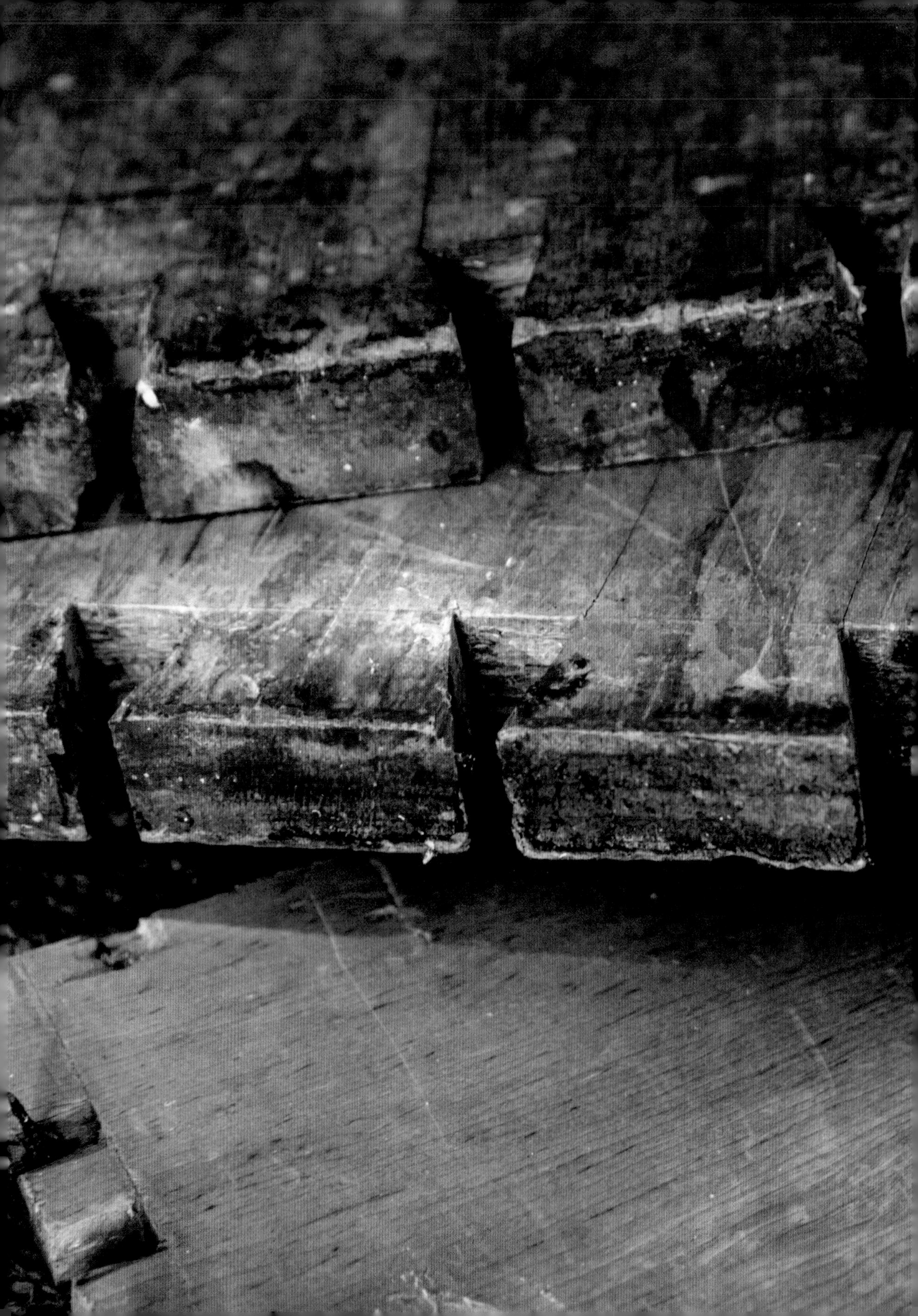

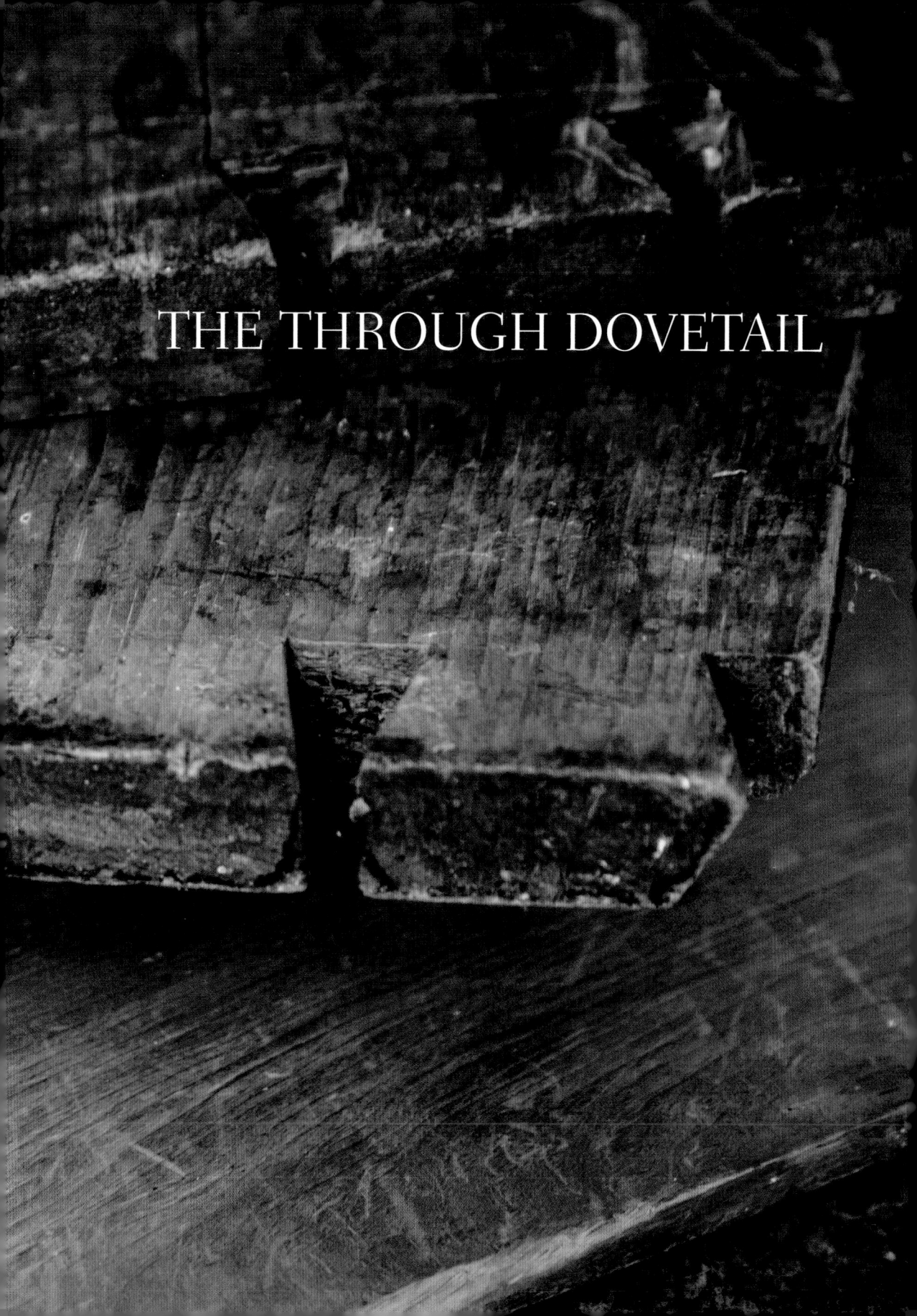

THE THROUGH DOVETAIL

If you need to join two boards at a right angle, and maximum strength is important, you're going to be cutting dovetails. There are other ways to make corners that survive the test of time (such as the nailed rabbet on page 132), but none are as strong as the dovetail.

The common through dovetail is most familiar for its use in joining the corners of chests. Sometimes the beauty of this joint seemed a matter of pride for the maker, but often it was painted over to obscure the wooden structure beneath. The dovetail has always been a practical joint.

If you're reading this book, I'm betting you're aware of the modern fetishism of dovetails. I won't deny my regard for a well-fitting joint, but I think it's important for our generation to get over it a bit. In my utopia, most folks would know how to cut rugged, workmanlike dovetails for everyday use. So, help me out here. Once you learn this skill, teach others how straightforward it can be.

Get yourself a couple 1x10s and follow along. Let's break this down.

Because you're joining two boards together, dovetails start with a transfer of measurement. Set your marking gauge to the first board's thickness. If your stock is machine-uniform, you can set the gauge's pin to exact thickness, but if there is slight irregularity, set the gauge a touch proud – this will leave your end grain protruding at assembly, making final cleanup predictable. In this instance, I set it for exact thickness.

Before you mark anything, it is important to have straight and squared ends on your boards. Use the gauge to transfer the thickness of the first board to the face of the second, registering off the end grain.

Tilt the top of the gauge toward you and pull the pin across both faces. Don't go crazy pressing the pin deep into the wood here. Slow, gentle passes are all you need. If this is your tail board, carry the gauge line around the edges too. Then transfer the thickness of the second board to both faces of the first. In most scenarios, these boards will be the same thickness, but you know what they say assuming does, don't you? If this is the pin board, don't bother scribing the edges.

The tail board needs the gauge line on the edges, but the pin board does not.

Here is a shop-made dovetail gauge. If you are particular about your dovetail angles, you'll love these things. If you're like me, you don't bother with them. I rarely use this one, because I like cutting these angles by eye. You'll see later why this can actually work.

There are tons of ways people lay out the spacing of their dovetails: You can use a pair of compasses, one of those fancy equal-distance layout tools, or calculation (shudder). Feel free to look up tutorials on those methods elsewhere, but I'll show you how I do it by eye. Resist the temptation to measure, because the ability to eyeball small distances is an important woodworking skill. And measuring means math.

On this 9"-wide board, let's make four tails. First, mark the outer edges of the outermost tails at approximately 3/4" from the edge with a pencil mark.

THE THROUGH DOVETAIL

Then using a block of wood (or a chisel, a square blade, or whatever appropriately sized object is at hand), gauge an even distance in from both outer pencil marks to define the width of your tails. You should now have four pencil marks, which define the locations of the two outer tails.

Place a light pencil mark in what appears to be the center between those tails. (You can check your guess with something at hand, if you feel compelled.)

Now, draw in four marks to designate the two inner tails, providing equal spacing between the tails that looks good to your eye. There's no wrong amount – just try to make them about the same. Obviously, the center space will span the center pencil mark.

Placing your dovetail saw on the end grain at the pencil marks, visually square the saw plate, and gently pull backward to establish shallow kerfs. Mark your waste with penciled Xs.

If you're using the dovetail gauge, now's the time to mark the angles, but I'll show you here how I instead cut them by eye. Trust me, I don't do this just so that I can show off – many period makers eyeballed these cuts without fastidious layout. And it's just way more fun.

To saw the four tails, you will have four cuts angled in one direction and four going the other. Cut the same-angled tail sides on all four before shifting to the other angle, because this helps with consistency.

Place your saw in the squared kerf, and tilt the saw over slightly. Conventional woodworking guides will tell you that softwood tails should have a slope of 1:6 – 1 unit of run to 6 units of rise – and hardwood tails should be slightly steeper at 1:8, but pre-industrial craftsmen seem to have missed that statute. In reality, the body of surviving period furniture shows a wide variety of angles executed in all kinds of wood, and they have held their boards together for centuries. I'm not saying these slopes are bad advice; it's just that they're not scripture.

THE THROUGH DOVETAIL

After the first four cuts are made, tilt the saw the opposite direction and continue to cut the next four.

As I mentioned, these angles are all slightly different, but once assembled in the context of a piece of furniture, you'll never be able to tell.

92   JOINED: A BENCH GUIDE TO FURNITURE JOINERY

Turn the board in the vise and saw off the waste outside the outer tails. Go carefully, making sure not to saw inside your baseline. If you want, saw the top edge and front together then flip the board around to saw the back and finish the cut.

Here's the finished cut.

Now you're ready to remove the waste between the tails. I'll show you two different ways to do this.

THE THROUGH DOVETAIL

The first method is by sawing the waste with a coping saw or turning saw.

Turn the blade so the teeth are aimed to the left and drop the saw blade into the right kerf of the waste to be removed. At about 1/8" above the baseline, turn the saw teeth into the waste and give a good push to start your kerf. Try to get down near your baseline as quick as possible, but be sure to stay off of it (on front and back) by at least 1/16". We'll be cleaning that up with a chisel later.

Saw all the way to the tail, being careful not to mar the outside face, which will be seen. Try to avoid scarring the inside face, but if you do, it's not catastrophic.

I'll use the last bit of waste to walk you through the other method of removal: chopping. Instead of sawing the waste away, I usually opt to chop when using thin softwood, such as that used in drawer sides. Sawing is a heck of a lot easier in thicker material and hardwood.

Lay the board on the bench with the dovetails above the bench's leg so that the force of every chop goes right to the floor instead of bouncing around. It really does make a difference. Make a chop with a mallet-driven chisel about 1/8" off the baseline.

Then use the chisel bevel-down to knock out a V-shaped chip. And no, your eyes do not deceive you: My board is not secured to the benchtop. This is because the chopping is primarily downward, not lateral. I find leaving the board free is a great help when I need to quickly clear material off the bench or make adjustments, because I never have to release and retighten clamps or holdfasts. As an aside, if you roughen your benchtop with a toothing plane, it considerably increases the grip on your stock. I can't imagine trying to secure work on one of those polished bowling-alley benchtops.

Here's the chopped V.

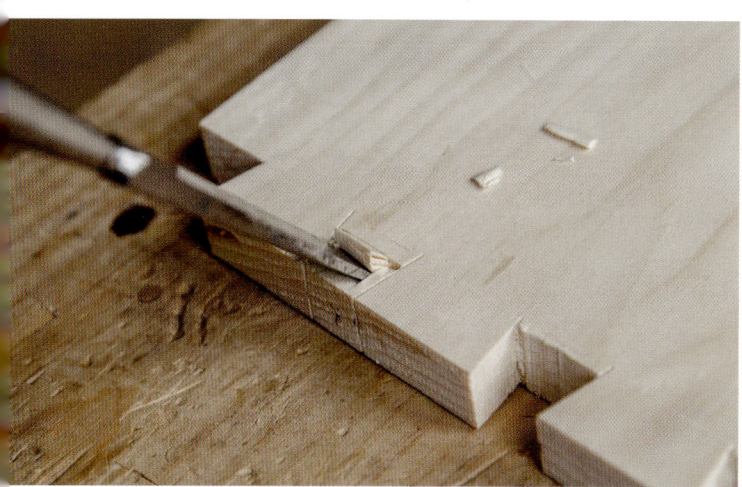

Repeat these steps a few more times to work toward half the thickness, being careful not to scar your sacred exterior dovetail slopes.

Once you're halfway through the thickness of the board, place your chisel half of the distance to the baseline and chop straight down. Then take half again of the remaining distance, leaving the tiniest line of waste above the baseline.

When you have a sliver of waste left, you can finally place the chisel's edge on the baseline. The first chop should be gentle, though, for accuracy's sake. Here's a standard pre-industrial technique that many modern woodworkers ignore: Undercut the waste between the tails. Unless you're a cyborg, establishing perfect 90° shoulders between tails is a waste of time. Tilt the chisel a few degrees off of 90° and chop to the halfway point.

Pine is pretty soft stuff and usually chips a bit at this stage, no matter how sharp your chisel. But good sharpening practices, and taking little bites at a time, help more than anything else. As you can imagine, historic examples are full of tear-out between tails.

THE THROUGH DOVETAIL

Wipe all the chips off the bench. Seriously, *all* of them, or you'll dent your precious board. Flip the board over on the clean benchtop to chop from the other side.

The only real difference on this side is that instead of chiseling a V, you can pop the chips from the end grain. I don't pop the chips on the first side so there's some support on the back at this step.

These let loose easily, so no need to drive the chisel too hard.

When you get halfway, the waste will break free. At this point you'll be happy your board isn't clamped down. Pick it up and knock the chunk out.

Finish chopping to the baseline as before. Repeat this whole process in the remaining sawn waste areas between tails.

Place the board in your vise to do a bit of cleanup.

Rest your non-dominant hand on the board with your index finger at the baseline. This allows you to rest your chisel on your finger rather than on the board. Pinch the chisel with that hand to maximize control of the cut.

Pare the hanging bits with gentle and controlled cuts. Watch all your sacred lines here – they're all around your chisel.

This is what the undercut V looks like with a backlit straightedge. The relief is not extreme – all that matters is that it's less than 90°. I have seen disassembled period dovetails that have considerably more relief, but a massive undercut is not necessary.

If the shoulders outside the tails need any touching up, do it now.

104   JOINED: A BENCH GUIDE TO FURNITURE JOINERY

Grab your pin board and put it in the vise, aligning the height to a block of scrap wood.

Slide the block to the back of the bench to support your tail board while scribing the tails. Looking from overhead, slide the tail board so that its baseline meets the inner face of the pin board. Don't just flush the end of the tails – it's the baseline that's important here. Use your finger to align the edges flush, pressing down firmly with your other hand. Don't rush this alignment and don't fudge anything – this step is make or break.

THE THROUGH DOVETAIL

When you're confident everything is perfectly lined up, scribe the angles with your knife. Several gentle and progressively deeper lines are better than one deep line. Do all the right sides first, then come back for the left sides, as you did with the sawing of the tails.

Now you can see why the angles of the dovetails do not need to match each other: the pins are perfectly scribed to their respective tails. This board is not interchangeable with any other board in the world now. Label your joint on the edges of both boards before separating them.

If you are having a hard time seeing the scribed lines on the end grain, you can use a wide chisel to deepen the line a touch. Some folks like to run a pencil inside the knife line. Do whatever you need to do to see those lines clearly. Making the first half of this joint has been relatively low key, but once your tails are scribed it's time to get persnickety.

With a small square, carry the scribed lines down the show face of the board.

Mark your waste.

The rule in our shop is, "When in pine, leave the line." So, set your saw on the waste side of the line. In hardwoods, you'll leave half of the line. In softwoods, you'll leave the whole line. This is because the members will compress into each other as they're driven tight.

Remove the waste as before, but don't forget that the angles are running front to back this time. The wider opening facing you is the exterior sacred side, but you don't want to start sawing into the pin at the far side either.

Chop the waste as before. Don't be tempted to go further than halfway, because you want the bottom of your undercut to be centered.

Now you can test the fit at the vise.

Areas that are too tight will readily reveal themselves. If the joint doesn't go at least halfway together with hand pressure, examine every area closely to see where things are getting hung up.

Notice how the outermost tail is scraping the pin a bit here.

Yep, that pin needs paring.

Pop quiz: In this scenario, which lines are the sacred lines? It's important that you know. The answer is the top and near edges. Therefore, if slight paring is required (as in this case), start the chisel below the top edge and keep all the work inside the joint. You should only ever pare sacred lines when you are 100% confident that the joint will not go together without it. But be careful messing with the sacred.

THE THROUGH DOVETAIL

Dovetails should be tight enough to need driving. Grab a softwood scrap to rap on with the mallet.

By the time you can close the joint past halfway with moderate pressure, you can feel confident it will close all the way.

To ease final assembly, chamfer all your secondary (inside) edges. Be 100% sure you understand what will be visible and what won't, or you'll kick yourself when you see that chamfer in the finished joint.

Chamfer the inside edges of the pins, starting *a bit below* the top, *not* starting right at the top. Do the same for the inside edge of the tails. If you aren't sure, put the joint back together to visualize what will be seen and what won't.

THE THROUGH DOVETAIL

Set the baseline on your pin board to the height of your handy support block, and slide the block to the back of the bench. Brush your glue on the insides of the joint. Yes, even on the undercut area.

114 JOINED: A BENCH GUIDE TO FURNITURE JOINERY

Drive the dovetails home with the mallet and the softwood scrap. Go slow and even. This is especially important for long joints.

If you need to pull the workpiece out of the vise to close gaps, go for it. When the glue's hot, do whatever you've got to do to get it right.

If there is a baseline gap that is driving you bonkers, don't be afraid to put a clamp on it. Otherwise, make sure it's square and walk away – it's not going anywhere while glue dries.

THE THROUGH DOVETAIL

After the joint has dried overnight, touch up your smoothing plane for the keenest edge you can manage. Flushing this joint requires a sharp tool and light touch. Set the plane's toe (front of the sole) on the board and make a quick, confident, skewed stroke. This should be a light cut or you risk tearing the grain when it reverses.

Whatever you do, don't plane from the other direction off the end, because you will break off the back side of the pin board.

If you have members protruding, pare them in a skewing motion with a razor-sharp chisel.

Stay sharp, light, and quick.

Plane the edges of the joint flush with a skewed stroke, coming around the corner.

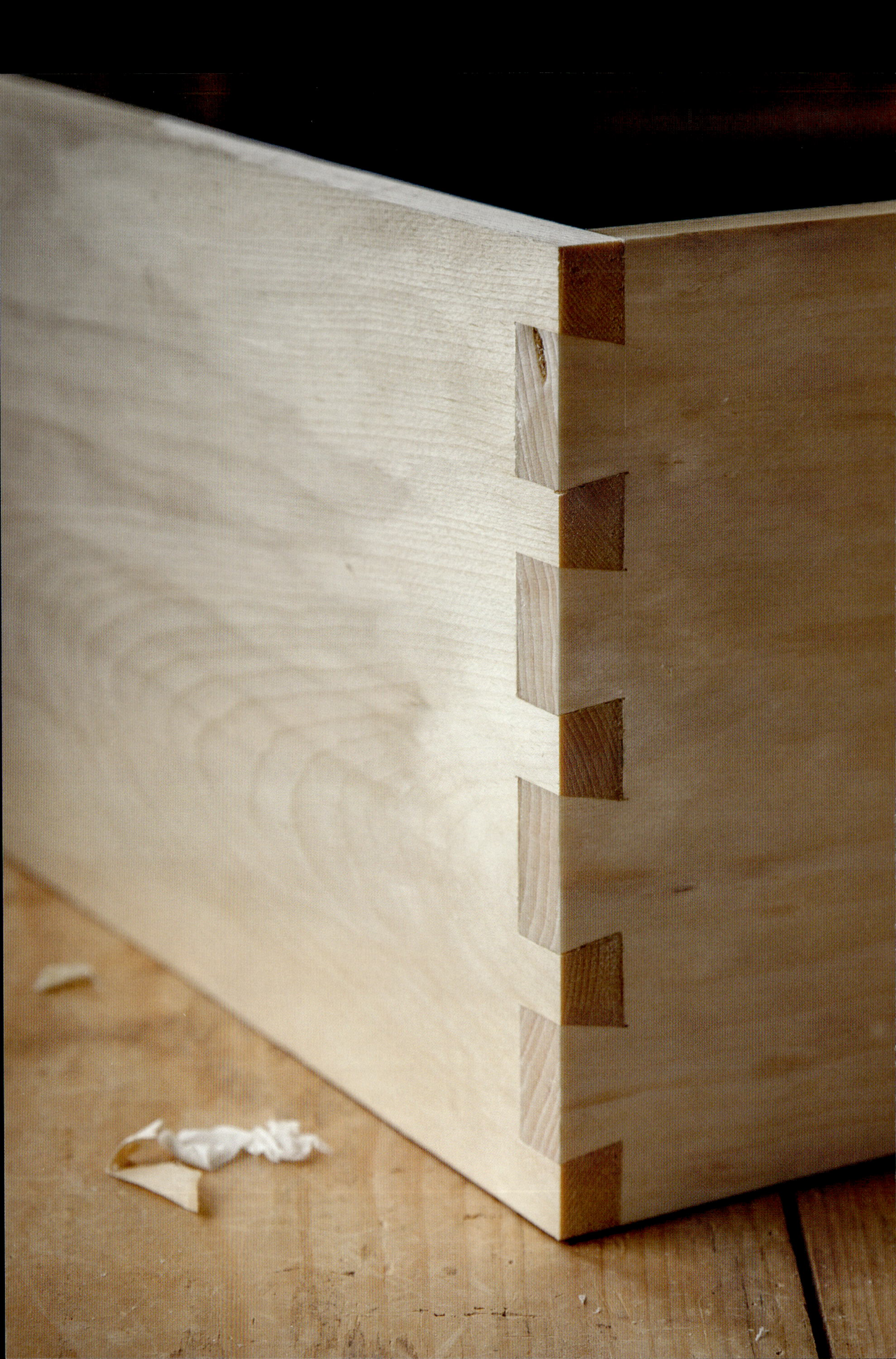

With this method, no measurements are needed.

Keep practicing. The only way to improve is to continue making stuff to the best of your ability.

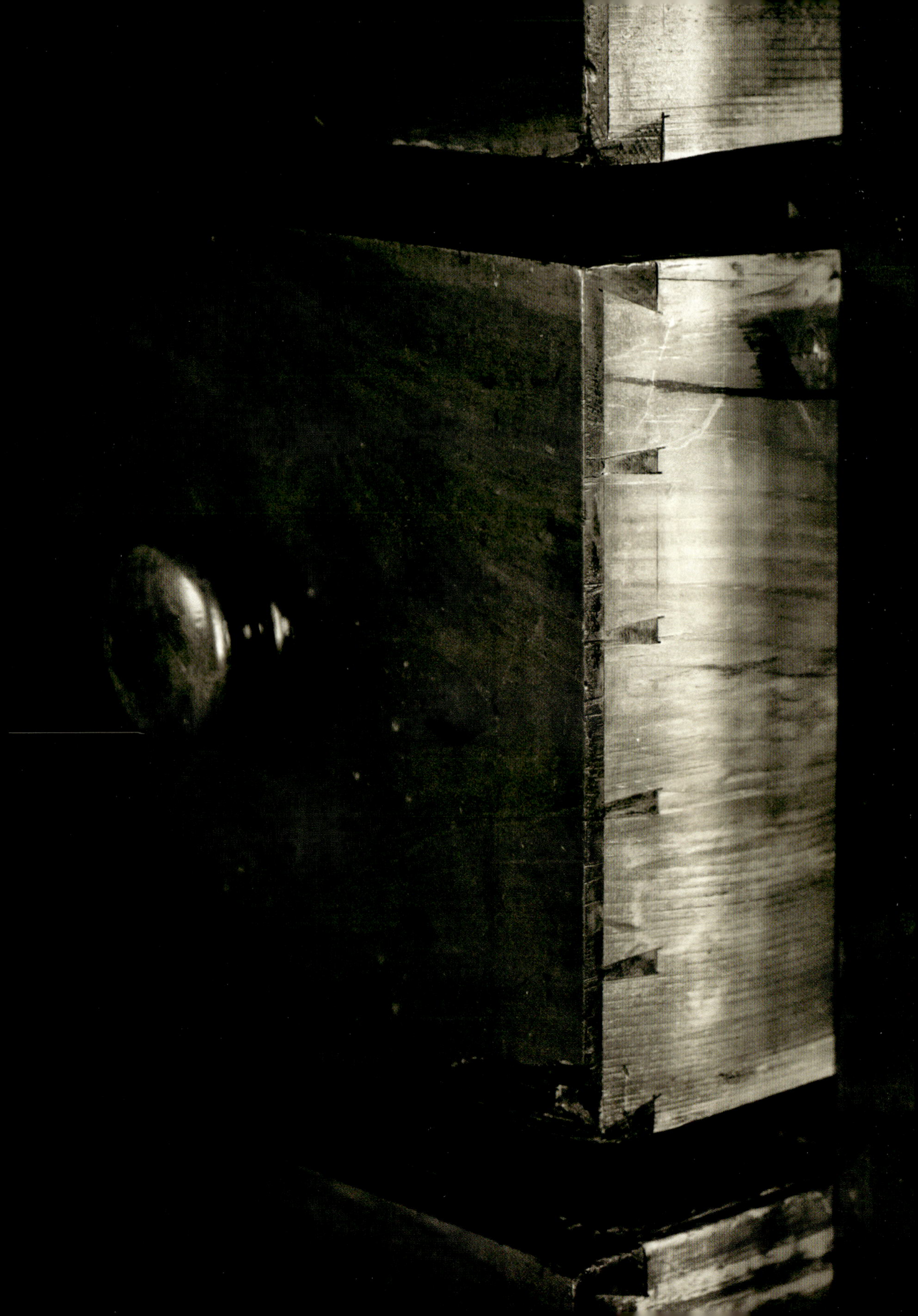

THE HALF-BLIND DOVETAIL

Half-blind dovetails are similar to through dovetails, so I will simply show you the aspects that are different. I'll be cutting this joint for a drawer front.

Start out by placing the 3/4"-thick drawer front in the vise. In this case, drawer fronts should be prepped to a uniform thickness, unlike our table rail, because we will be referencing off the inside face to gauge a baseline shy of the exterior face. The distance doesn't matter, as long as the tails are tall enough and there's at least 1/8" material to the front edge.

Scribe the line.

Then scribe that same baseline distance on your 5/8"-thick drawer side to lay out and cut your dovetails.

Fancy, small-pinned dovetails are classically beautiful, but cleanup between those tails is tricky. Be careful and use the tiniest chisel you've got. Use your knife if you have to.

Also note in the image above that the tail to the right is a half tail, which will hide a groove plowed for the drawer bottom. I won't be showing you the drawer bottom here, but at least you understand what's going on.

Make sure you line up the drawer side's baseline to the inner face of the drawer front – don't bring the tails all the way flush to the outside. Those tiny pins make scribing trickier.

124   JOINED: A BENCH GUIDE TO FURNITURE JOINERY

The end grain of hardwood gives a nice, clean surface for scribing.

Gauge the thickness of the drawer side to transfer to the inside of the drawer face. But set the gauge a hair proud so that the drawer side actually sits deeper than is strictly necessary. (This helps with fitting the drawer and prevents the sides from sticking during seasonal swelling.) My gauge's pin is made from a 1/16" drill bit. Because the cutting edge is centered, I can set my pin on the surface of the wood, and that half-of-a-drill-bit thickness (1/32") is enough to make the drawer side sink just below flush.

Saw the pins free. This is very different than the process of cutting through dovetails, because the saw cannot pass through the front of the workpiece. So turn the drawer face sideways in the vise and lean it back diagonally as pictured. This position is useful in helping to clearly see what's going on here, and also because you will be sawing well below the interior baseline to clear as much material out of the tails' pockets as possible.

Yes, these saw kerfs will be seen on the inside when the drawer is opened, but sawing these overcuts has been a common practice for a long time. This bothers modern woodworkers, but I like how pragmatic the approach is – it makes cutting the joint much easier. Note that the drawer face's end grain is the place admirers ogle the most – there's no overcutting permitted, because every line is sacred.

The pocket for the half tail at the bottom can also be sawn some, but you don't have much space to work with here. Most of the waste will have to be chopped out.

To chop the waste between the pins, lay the board on the bench. If you have a wall handy, butt it against the wall.

The chopping will all be done from this side, so you don't need to make that V-pocket. Just pop the chips out. The only difference is that you have to advance in pieces because the chips will get trapped by the inward-sloping walls. I just turn my chisel on the diagonal and take small pieces out at a time.

128   JOINED: A BENCH GUIDE TO FURNITURE JOINERY

The baseline can be carefully pared at the vise.

The half-tail pocket can be split out some, but most of it is chopping work. This is the slowest step, but don't get impatient – all of this is fragile.

The finished drawer face with pins.

Chamfer the inside of the tails as before. You can also chamfer the bottom of the tail end, because it will be hidden. If you need to plow a groove for a drawer bottom, now's the time to do it.

Coat all the inside surfaces thoroughly with glue, and drive the joint together.

Here's the inside of the assembled joint with the offending saw kerfs. Gnarly, right? To my eye, there is a certain workmanlike beauty about this.

The half-blind dovetail. I hope you've seen that though there are a few differences from the through dovetail, it is essentially the same process.

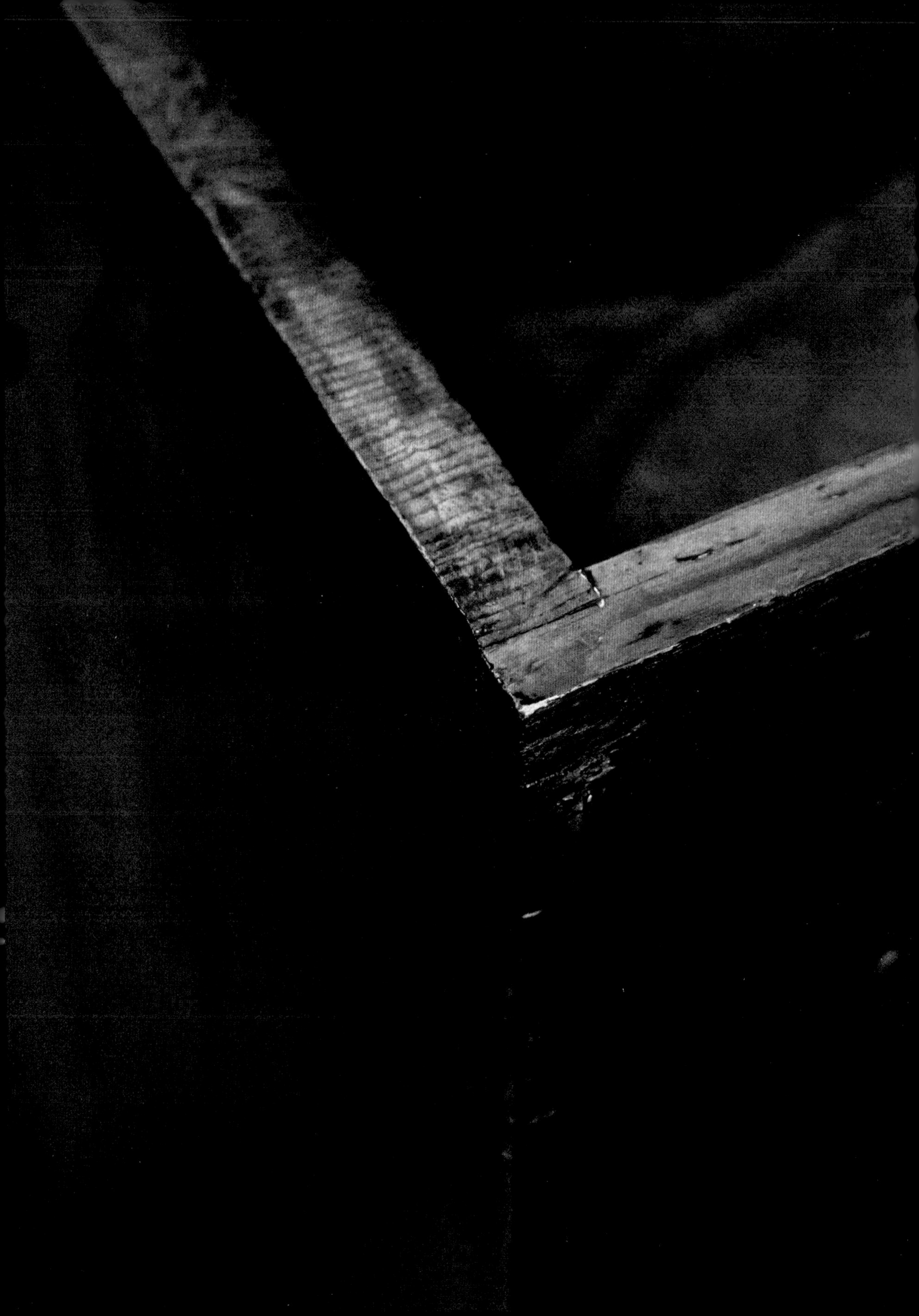

THE NAILED RABBET

The nailed rabbet is one of the oldest and most basic woodworking joints, but its utility was not lost on the succeeding generations. This joint was, in fact, the most common method of constructing chests for budget-minded, pragmatic customers throughout the 19th century. However, in modern times the nailed joint has fallen into disrepute, owing largely to unfortunate experience with cheap boxes slapped together with modern wire nails.

But this contemporary prejudice ignores the beauty and strength of legit blacksmith-made nails. In fact, this joint is a great opportunity to support local smiths. Or to learn to make your own nails.

There are two ways to cut this joint that I will show you. The first method is quick, but because it depends on a specialty tool, I will also demonstrate that it can be done with a more basic kit.

The moving fillister plane is a specialized tool that has several different features for regulating the final result of the rabbet. It has a "nicker" (a cutting blade that scores across the wood fibers in front of the plane's iron), a brass depth stop, and a wooden fence. All of these features are adjustable, but like any highly regulated tool, setup is a bit of a time investment, and any piece not perfectly dialed in adds fiddling time. (There is not space in this tutorial to cover all of the factors of fillister troubleshooting and adjustment – we'll look at that in a future lesson.) So, if you're cutting a bunch of rabbets of the same dimension, a moving fillister is the bee's knees. If you've only got a couple, you're better off doing it by hand and eye.

Like all fenced tools, the success of the moving fillister is largely dependent on the accuracy of the stock prep. The ends *must* be square.

134   JOINED: A BENCH GUIDE TO FURNITURE JOINERY

The width of your rabbet should exceed the thickness of the board it will join by at least 1/4". This overlap will help mitigate splitting when you drive the nails, and will get trimmed off later.

Start at the far end of the board with your left hand pressing the fence against the board. Gently draw the plane backward to scribe the shoulder line with the nicker. Then, starting about halfway down the rabbet, push the plane forward with your right hand while your left hand presses the fence against the board.

Continue making confident passes, focusing on holding the fence against the board. You don't need to press down as much as you need to press in on the fence.

THE NAILED RABBET

The shavings will eject out onto the board. Keep them cleared away from the plane as it does its work.

This is the proper hand position for a moving fillister plane: right hand on the back pushing forward and left hand pushing the fence into the board. Don't try to do both jobs with both hands. They each only have one job.

The rabbet is cut fast with this method, so make sure you're keeping an eye on depth and squareness (i.e. that you're not tipping the plane out of square). The rabbet's interior does not have to be pristine and free of flaws, because it's hidden inside the joint.

The joint is complete in one straightforward operation. Almost all of the energy investment is in plane setup and adjustment.

The second way to cut this joint requires nothing but the most basic kit: a knife, a square, a gauge, a saw, and a chisel. First, scribe the depth of the rabbet on the inside face. In period nailed chests, they are rarely deeper than 1/4"; most are closer to 1/8".

Use a long square to lay out a shoulder line with your knife. Score deep – this is your sacred line.

Carry the shoulder line over the edges to meet the gauge line.

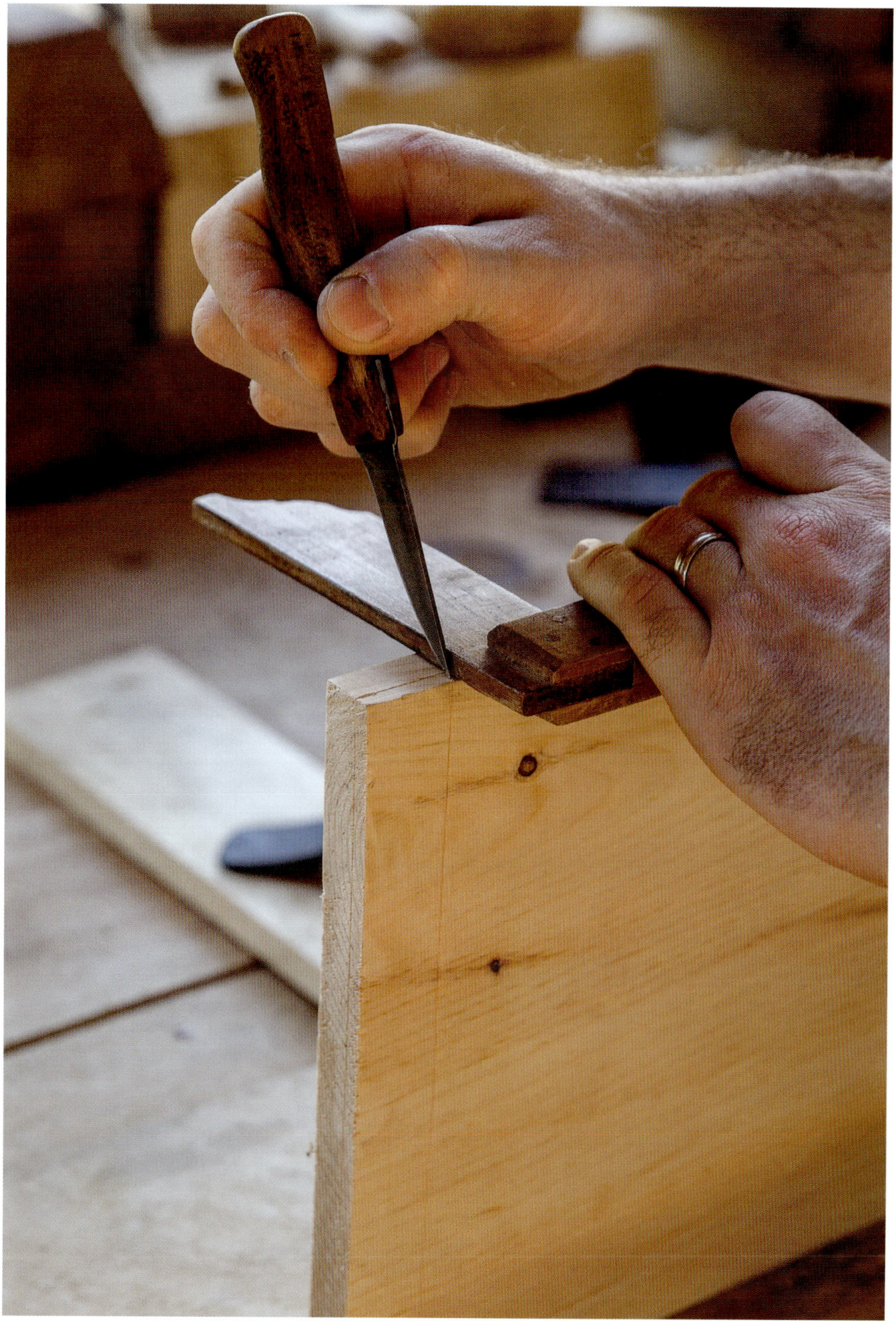

To keep that shoulder line nice and crisp, carve a shallow V, as you did when cutting the square tenon's exterior shoulder.

A chisel tilted at just the right angle enables you to zip through that line in one fell swoop. The more you practice this step, the less finicky it becomes, but the first few times you do this it will involve lots of starts and stops. Keep at it.

Place the saw's teeth down into the groove and begin sawing, being mindful not to let the saw jump out of the kerf. Also, watch to make sure you're sawing square. A slight undercut is not desirable here because it would be seen in the final joint, but it would be better than inadvertently tilting the saw in the opposite direction, leaving an unsightly gap inside the joint.

It is a common mistake to saw the ends of the rabbet deeper than the middle. To offset this tendency, use the first few teeth of the saw to deepen the middle a bit.

Use a wide chisel to pop the waste from the end grain. Start at half depth to see which way the grain wants to run. If it runs down close to the gauge line, you will not want to split much further. The rest should be carefully pared cross grain. Don't wale on the chisel as you're splitting – little force is necessary.

In this instance, you can see the split is actually running up. This is better than running down. This means I can safely chisel the waste away.

Continue splitting down the length of the board, but watch for changes in grain direction. It is not uncommon to have one end split up and the other down.

You could pare this rabbet to final depth with a wide chisel, or use a skewed rabbet plane to clean it up. The rabbet plane is like a moving fillister without the fence, depth stop, and nicker. Using it is a freehand operation that requires attention to the gauge lines.

This method makes rabbets just as clean as the fillister method. Because I rarely do large runs of the same-size rabbet at a time, I usually use this second method in my shop.

Now to join the two boards. Place the square-end board in the vise a touch higher than a support block and place the rabbeted board into place on top, just as you did with the dovetails. Make sure there are no unsightly gaps and make any necessary adjustments now.

Get yourself some legit handmade nails from a blacksmith. If you don't know a local smith, a quick internet search will pull up some options. Many smiths don't feel like making nails because most customers balk at the somewhat expensive cost per piece, so if you find a kind soul who will set you up with nails, treat 'em good. As an alternative, haunt antique stores and flea markets for boxes of old fasteners. Cut nails are relatively common, but you can occasionally find hand-wrought examples in reusable condition too.

The size of your pilot holes is very important. Find a bit the diameter of the nail one third of the way past the tip. In pine, this is enough clearance for driving, but still ensures a firm bite into the wood. In hardwoods, you may want to relieve the very top of the hole a little bigger, but testing on scrap wood will tell you all you need to know.

Gently scribe the centerline of the board below onto the face of the rabbeted board, then eyeball even nail spacing. Make sure you're no closer than 1" to the ends of the joint. I chose to use three nails on this 9"-wide board; the number of nails depends on your stock width.

Remove the rabbeted board and bore the pilot holes at a slight angle inward as shown. When the nails are driven like this, they are less liable to work loose over the years of seasonal fluctuation and heavy use. The center hole is also at a slight angle, but it doesn't matter which direction.

Place the rabbet back on the other board to mark the pilot hole positions. Firmly holding the joint in position, place the bit into the first pilot hole and gently turn it in the hole. If you happen to have three arms, you're in luck. If not, just hold the drill by the wheel, and it's not too big a deal. Clamping this is easier, but I try to develop the ability to work without clamps in as many scenarios as possible, because I like the freedom that comes with adaptability. The photo at left shows what the first mark looks like.

Bore the pilot hole a little less than the full length of the nail's shaft at the same angle as before. Fortunately, there is a wide tolerance in this step – the angle never needs to be measured. Put the joint together and drive the first nail until it bites both boards together, but no further. Handwrought nails are square-shanked, making orientation irrelevant.

If you're using cut nails (shown right), orientation is everything. The cut nail's wedge shape must never be oriented across the grain of the rabbeted board, or it will be sure to split it. Think about how you would split a board with an axe: the wedge shape of the axe's bevel would run with the grain. But you don't want to split this board, so turn the wedge *with* the grain (left nail shown), *not across* the grain (right nail shown).

THE NAILED RABBET 147

Mark the second pilot hole the same way as before, making sure you're pulling the joint tightly closed.

Then remove the rabbeted board and bore the second hole at an opposing angle to the first.

If you're gluing, now's the time. Once you're happy, drive the two nails all the way home.

Then the last hole can be bored and the nail driven without all the back-and-forth fuss of the first two.

Now that the joint is assembled, all that's left is to cut the overhang and smooth it flush. Knife a line up both edges in plane with the other board.

Then connect those two lines with a straightedge. Do not try to use a square – it's safer to connect the marks from both sides.

Saw the end flush with a fine saw, leaving it a hair proud to pare or plane smooth.

I tend to pare flush from the inside out before planing from the outside in. This method prevents "spelching," or breaking out at the end grain.

The finished rabbet joint. Who doesn't love showing off handmade nails?

THE NAILED RABBET 151

"THE DADO"

Dadoes are commonly used for shelves and drawer runners fit into cases, as well as other miscellaneous items. When bookshelves are maxed out with weight, dadoes provide extra engagement and support to the shelf. It is possible to butt and nail a shelf in place, and you can even nail a cleat underneath it if you want. But utilizing the dado will make for a much stronger, as well as more attractive, shelf.

This lesson will be similar to the nailed rabbet tutorial, in that I will show you two ways to cut this joint: with a dedicated plane, or by saw and chisel. Although most dado planes I've seen feature depth stops, the tendency for these to slip in use is a real concern. Because of this propensity, I use a gauged line instead of a depth stop. (This note of caution could also apply to the fillister plane, by the way.) Because the setup for using a dado plane is quite straightforward, and the fact that without it, you must execute two sacred saw cuts, I prefer making dadoes with the plane rather than cutting them with a saw – even for small batches.

I'll be showing you a couple joints for a bookshelf made out of 7/8"-thick pine.

Scribe the dado's depth with your gauge. These are anywhere between 1/8" to 1/4", but no need to go any deeper or the board will be significantly weakened.

Depth gauged on the edge of the board.

Square and secure a scrap-wood guide fence for the dado plane. I use my holdfasts for quick attachment and adjustment.

THE DADO 155

There are two nickers on the dado plane, one for each side of the iron. Make sure these are good and sharp or you will have ragged edges around your shelves.

Press the dado plane against the fence at the far side of the board, and gently pull backward so that the two nickers can score the path.

Once the scored lines have defined the path, begin planing at the far end as with the rabbet, then continue to evenly remove material down the whole length of the dado. If one area is higher than the rest (likely your near side), take a few short passes just in that spot to even it all out.

As you move along, you should see continuous curls such as below. This is the result of a hefty cut with a sharp, skewed iron.

Once you hit your baseline on both sides, make sure you don't have a hump in the middle. If you do, plane only the hump until it disappears. That's it.

Here's how to do it without a specialty tool. First, square a line.

Using your board as a reference, mark the dado width a little narrower than the board. Don't shoot for exactness here or you'll regret it (and have a loose joint).

Square the lines across the face and down over the edges to meet the gauge line.

Because there are two lines to cut, you will have to carve a V into both sides.

160   JOINED: A BENCH GUIDE TO FURNITURE JOINERY

Start your saw at the far end as you did with the squared-tenon shoulder and with the rabbet. Then kerf the end near you.

Connect the two kerfs and make long, steady saw cuts, being careful not to jump out of the kerf.

There are four details to always be watching in this step: 1. Make sure you're sawing square at all times. 2. Don't go past the far gauge line. 3. Don't go past the near gauge line. 4. Keep your saw safely in the kerf. That's a lot to keep track of for such a simple-looking operation. Go slow and pay attention.

THE DADO 161

It always involves leaning over to check progress...

and crouching down in front.

Stop at the gauge line, then saw the second line.

Use a chisel narrower than the dado with the bevel facing down to remove the bulk of the waste out of the sawn area. Don't try to take huge bites at a time or you're liable to chip the sacred edges that you just cut so carefully. Pare to the gauge line from both ends with the chisel bevel-up, leaving the middle for the next step.

Once the dado is to depth at the ends, we've got to get the hump out of the middle.

You can finish the dado's depth with the chisel, but the router plane is essentially a jigged chisel set to a specific depth. It's a handy tool for this operation. You can set the depth of cut by placing the cutting edge into the dado at the far end and tapping the iron down until it bottoms. You can then use that setting to clear out the middle.

Because you're planing cross-grain, it's beneficial to skew the iron in the cut. This also helps the edge get into the corners of the dado to clear it out.

164   JOINED: A BENCH GUIDE TO FURNITURE JOINERY

Keep working the hump out, lifting a bit if there's too much meat in front of the iron.

To finish, work in from the other side – don't just go all the way across, or you risk breaking out the grain.

Make sure to thoroughly clean out the corners of the dado before putting the router away.

The finished sawn dado is just as clean as the one formed by the dado plane.

Now show the shelf board to the dado. It should be a hair too thick. Rather than planing the entire board to thickness, just plane the area to be fit – this is the easiest method, and it's got a long track record in woodworking history. Stabilizing a board for this cross-grain planing can be a headache because of the need to check the fit after every few passes, so I just sit on it. It's quick to check and sit back down. This process would be quite tedious if I had to clamp and unclamp every few passes.

The underside of the shelf will have a slight bevel at the joint.

The bevel underneath will be a little fuzzy from cross-grain planing, but if it fits nice and tight at the face, that's all that matters.

If you can see the bevel on the edge of the shelf, simply plane the underside of the front edge to make it a straight line.

The shelf is solid even without the glue and nails it will receive when the bookshelf is assembled.

afterword

I hope the tutorials in this book have proven to be a help to you. As I worked my way through these joints and sat down to put words to the techniques I've learned over the years, I tried to keep one aim in mind: to present this material in as clear and straightforward a way as possible. *Joined* is not intended to be simply a pretty woodworking book to occupy space on your bookshelf. It's not a collector's volume that ought to be kept in pristine and "as new" condition. Nor is it meant for coffee tables, nightstands, or armchairs. It's meant for the shop.

As you read through these chapters, I hope you've done more than simply nod along. It's a great thing to daydream about woodworking; the only problem is, not much gets accomplished that way. So if you haven't already mastered the concepts and skills presented in this book, I encourage you to bring it to your workbench and take the time to walk through these lessons alongside me. Once you give yourself the opportunity to cultivate the same skills that craftsmen have practiced for centuries, your shop work will gain new meaning and purpose as your confidence grows.

I claim no originality for the techniques in this book – nor do I think any of the material is particularly clever. This is old-school craftsmanship, plain and simple. It is the set of skills that is the foundation for every furniture project you will tackle.

If you're like many of us, as you read these words, your tools are out in your shop waiting for you. They're tucked away in your tool chest, sharp and ready for work, but there never seems to be enough time to get out there to make shavings. Go now. Set this book on your benchtop, and start at the beginning. Let the corners of this book be dinged and its pages be dog-eared. And let it always be filled with sawdust.

Build that chest from those boards you've been saving. Make that table for your daughter's graduation present. Create the kind of joinery that will last beyond your lifetime.

Go make something.

acknowledgments

I would like to extend my heartfelt gratitude to several individuals who have supported me in various ways in this work of research, experimentation, and writing: First and foremost, my lovely wife, Julia. Her commitment to keeping our family's ecology vibrant and steady is a constant source of inspiration to me. Our three boys are so full of enthusiasm for exploring this big, beautiful world in large part because of her influence.

I am indebted to Michael Updegraff and Grace Cox, my colleagues at *Mortise & Tenon*. Mike and Grace both take sincere ownership of their roles in *M&T*, and this seat-of-our-pants publishing venture would be impossible without their skill and dedication. Mike has edited this book, and the text was honed with his astute wordsmithing. I will always owe a profound appreciation to my copy editor, Megan Fitzpatrick, for all her years working with me on *M&T*. Her work on this book has only sunk me deeper into her debt.

I would be remiss to overlook the woodworking mentors who inspired me early on in my career. Mitch Kohanek and Donald C. Williams were the first to introduce me to the intricacies of historic furniture, and it was the infectious passion of these two men that inspired me to dedicate my life to pursuing a deeper understanding of historic craftsmanship. I would also like to thank Christopher Schwarz and Peter Follansbee. The methods of research they've developed for their work have been the primary inspirations and models for the development of my own. My conversations with Chris and Peter over the years have brought fruitful refinement to my methods and conclusions.

I am grateful to the furniture restoration clients who entrusted their furniture to my studio's care over the years. Without this daily exposure to handcrafted objects, my understanding of pre-industrial methods would be built on the sand of assumptions and conjecture. I've also benefited from the generosity of numerous museums that have granted me particularly intimate access to their collections. Eric Litke at the Yale University Art Gallery's Furniture Study, Charles Hummel at the Winterthur Museum, Shelley Cathcart at Old Sturbridge Village, Brad Emerson at the Jonathan Fisher House, and Angela Waldron at the Farnsworth Art Museum have donated many hours to facilitate my analysis of the artifacts in their collections. These research trips have proven to be an invaluable resource to draw from while formulating theories of pre-industrial cabinetmaking process.

And a heartfelt "Thank you" is again due to the loyal subscribers of *Mortise & Tenon*. Not only does your support uphold our continued research and publishing efforts, it also puts food in the bellies of our young, growing families. We are indebted to you all.

glossary

arris the sharp intersection of two surfaces, the edge

auger a spiral bit with a screw lead and cutters for boring wood

baseline the line that marks the bottom of a joint

bench hook a metal planing stop filed with teeth that is mortised into the workbench top

bevel the sloped angle on the end of a cutting tool

brace a U-shaped tool that rotates bits for boring into wood

cabinetmaker a historic term for a furniture maker

chamfer an angled slope (usually 45°) at the intersection of two surfaces

cheek the wide, flat side of a tenon

chisel a metal cutting tool with a beveled edge

drawbore the method in which intentionally offset holes are brought together when a pin is driven through them

end grain the surface across the growth rings of a board, the end of a board

facet small, flat planes left from a cutting tool

gauge/marking gauge a tool used to scribe a line parallel to the fence

hide glue an adhesive made from collagen, derived from the hides of cattle and other animals

horn extra material left at the end of a piece to be mortised

jig a device that guides a cutting tool's action in an effort to regulate the outcome

joinery methods used to connect wooden members

kerf the groove made by a saw

layout marks on a workpiece designating the locations of essential features

mallet a wooden-headed striking tool

mortise an excavation in wood that receives the tenon of a mating component

mortise-and-tenon joint a joint consisting of an excavation in one piece of wood and a corresponding projection in another

paring cutting away the edge or outer surface, typically with a chisel bevel-down

pin (on a gauge) a thin metal point used to scratch the wood surface

pin (wooden) a thin wooden nail used to secure a joint together

plane (smoothing, fore) a tool that creates a flat plane by means of a cutting iron secured with a wedge

rail a horizontal member of a table that joins into the legs

reference face the flat and smooth surface of wood on which marking and measuring tools are registered

sacred (edge, face, line) a visible portion of a finished object which, once established, must be left pristine

saw, back a saw with a stiffened top edge used for fine woodworking

saw, coping a U-shaped frame that holds a thin blade taut for cutting curves

saw, crosscut a saw sharpened to smoothly cut across the grain

saw, dovetail a small rip-filed backsaw intended for cutting the sloped sides of dovetails

saw, rip a saw sharpened to cut efficiently with the grain

saw, tenon a backsaw intended for cutting the cheeks of tenons

saw, turning a wooden-framed saw with a thin blade intended to cut curves, but is larger than a coping saw

shoulder a step perpendicular to the face of the member of a joint

side rest a wooden hook-shaped device for securing work while crosscutting

skew cutting at an oblique angle

square a tool used to measure and mark 90°

squeeze-out a small amount of adhesive that emerges from a joint upon assembly

stretcher a horizontal chair member connecting the bottoms of legs

tail the fan-shaped member of a dovetail joint

tenon a projection cut into a wooden member, intended to join into a mortise

turner a craftsperson who turns objects on a lathe

undercut a tilted cut under the layout line of a joint, utilized to ensure a tight fit on the show surface

vise a screw-driven workshop device for holding material while working it

waste the material to be removed

other titles by this author

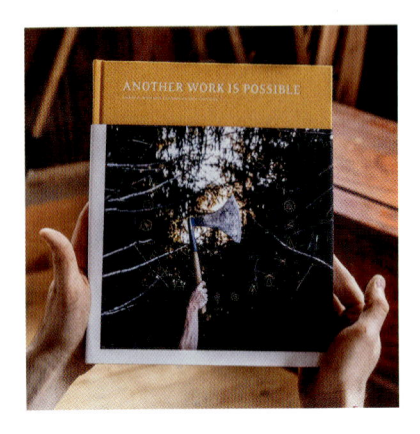

Another Work is Possible

Mortise & Tenon, 2020

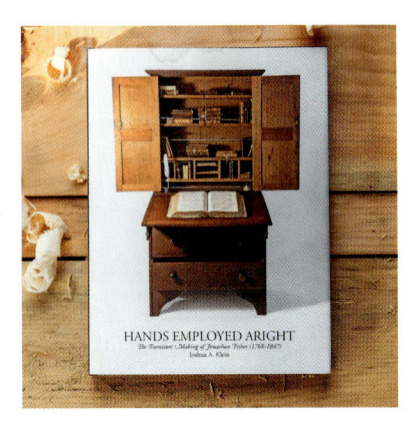

Hands Employed Aright: The Furniture Making of Jonathan Fisher (1768-1847)

Lost Art Press, 2018

Apprenticeship Series Instructional Video: *Tables*

Mortise & Tenon, 2017

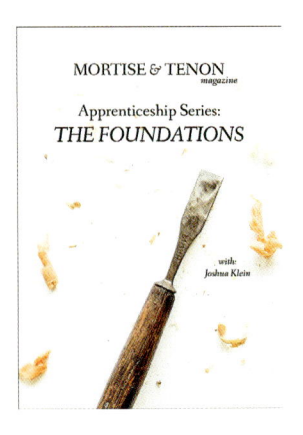

Apprenticeship Series Instructional Video: *The Foundations*

Mortise & Tenon, 2016

available at:
http://mortiseandtenonmag.com